# NEW GODDESS ON MOUNT PAEKTU

# NEW GODDESS ON MOUNT PAEKTU

## MYTH AND TRANSFORMATION IN NORTH KOREAN LANDSCAPE

ROBERT WINSTANLEY-CHESTERS

First published 2020
by Black Halo Productions

ISBN 978-1-8380702-0-5 (paperback)
ISBN 978-1-8380702-1-2 (ebook)

A catalogue record for this book is available
from the British Library

The publisher has no responsibility for the continued existence or accuracy of URLs for
external or third-party internet websites referred to in this book, and does not guarantee that
any content on such websites is, or will remain, accurate or appropriate

Typeset by BBR Design, Sheffield

# Contents

# Abstract

North Korea's 2015 New Year's Address was replete with references to Mt Paektu, the highest mountain on the Korean peninsula, and to 2015 being the seventieth anniversary of the Liberation of the Korean peninsula from Japanese occupation. Two years later, 2017 saw the centennial anniversary of the birth of Kim Jong Suk, first wife of Kim Il Sung, mother of Kim Jong Il and grandmother of Kim Jong Un. It is perhaps not surprising that at these celebratory moments the landscapes central to Korean mountain cults, ancient and modern, come to the fore. This book suggests considering contemporary North Korean ideology and the importance of the Kim dynasty as having evolved from traditional Korean mountain beliefs and practices, centred on Mt Paektu. It examines the common cultural roots of modern North and South Korean mountain legend and suggests a certain methodological grid for its analysis. While much of the legend surrounding Kim Il Sung's guerrilla resistance in the forests and valleys around Mt Paektu is determinedly masculine, Kim Jong Suk constitutes an authoritative female presence. As a bodyguard of Kim Il Sung and a champion of revolutionary struggle, Kim Jong Suk transcends both her defined gender role and her human nature. In order to transform from the young peasant girl into a great Revolutionary Mother and a symbol of the charismatic power of the Kim dynasty, Kim Jong Suk has to undergo difficult and painful trials and toils. In this recounting of her struggle Kim Jong Suk is both transfigured by and herself transfigures the terrain of the mountain, becoming a key player in the transformation of its slopes into the charismatic mythography of the North Korean present.

# Note about Romanisation

Romanisation is one of the greatest challenges when it comes to coherent writing and scholarship focused on the Korean peninsula. There are currently at least four separate romanisation strategies for converting Korean Hangeul (한글) or Chosŏn'gŭl (조선) script into an English-language context. Both Koreas, of course, use entirely different approaches and have changed these approaches over time. North Korean romanisation style refers to Pyongyang and Kim Il Sung, whereas South Korea's current Revised Romanisation strategy (in its 2008 form), refers to Pyeongyang and Kim Il-song. There is an extraordinary amount of politics and ideology in the use of these different strategies and it is an issue for all scholars when quoting from text produced in both current Korean nations to either choose one over the other, or to Romanise according to the source of the quotation, place name, person or text. This book, therefore, adopts a strategy as far as possible of objective multiplicity. This, of course, inevitably breaks all the usual patterns of uniformity in documents and is contested as a technique, certainly not problematic, nor free of ideology or presumption. In the case of historical Korean names, places, concepts and nations, the book uses the McCune–Reischauer romanisation strategy created in 1937 by George McCune of the University of California, Berkeley, and Edwin Reischauer of Harvard University. While McCune essentially crystallises some of the political imperialism, academic elitism and Orientalism of the twentieth century and complicates written Korean with judicious and at times excessive use of diacritic marks, it is a comprehensive system of romanisation that avoids the politics and ideology of the present. When using Korean names, places and concepts in North Korea, the book uses the North Korean romanisation strategy. When using Korean names, places and concepts in South Korea the book uses the Revised Romanisation strategy from 2008. On occasion when a term or name is important to both, on the first instance in a chapter the book includes both romanisations. Following the tradition instigated by Professor David Mason, the book uses the spelling *sanshin* for traditions of Korean mountain deities, and *sanshingak* for their places of veneration. These are only capitalised at the beginning of a sentence and have no plural nor separate gendered forms.

# Acknowledgements and Background to this Book

Every academic monograph of course has a long story about the research and writing that lays behind it, but the book you have in your hands or on your screen has certainly travelled a circuitous, complicated path, perhaps metaphorically as circuitous and complicated as some of the journeys the new goddess of Mt Paektu that it is focused on would have traversed. From the date that the contract for this book was offered, 24 April 2015, it has been more than five years to the date it structurally was completed, 17 May 2020. Conceptually it has not travelled perhaps as far as its author would have liked or imagined, but emotionally and geographically the voyage has been long and the transformation of the book itself great. I want to acknowledge at the very outset that originally this book was supposed to be co-authored and that two goddesses and two sets of mythology should have been involved, crossing the 38th parallel with legends and transformations from both sides of the Korean peninsula. Co-authoring is, as anyone who has tried to do it, extremely hard, and in this case ultimately it proved impossible. While the two stories of transformation this book was supposed to tell are certainly recountable in a single body of text, for personal and intellectual reasons it was not possible on this occasion. During the early months of 2020, including the global series of lockdowns and isolations due to the Covid-19 pandemic, the now sole author of this book spent many weeks disconnecting the entwined stories in the original version of the manuscript, and stripping out the work of his co-author and the extraordinary legend focused on by them. No doubt they will one day publish a fantastic monograph on their legend, to which they are powerfully and emotionally committed, but it won't be co-authored with me. However, the author of this book by trade is a Human Geographer, and any quick glance through these pages will tell the reader that there is much more in here than the theoretical and conceptual frames of Human Geography. So I absolutely acknowledge the inspiration of my former co-author, Victoria Ten (sometimes known as Jeonhwa Jeon), and the many hours of work that she (and her esteemed mother, known only to me as Dr Burman), put into this project. I have as much as possible deconstructed the text as we last worked together on it, so that I can, without embarrassment, claim ownership and copyright of this material as it connects to Kim Jong Suk, but absolutely acknowledge Chapter Three as a shared act of co-production. Victoria's love of Foucault and theories of East Asian immortals and self-transformations was profoundly influential for me, and as difficult as this process has been I thank her genuinely for all of her energy, intelligence and commitment. For readers wanting a powerful study of practices of self-cultivation, I recommend Victoria's doctoral thesis, completed in 2017 at Leiden University: "Body and Ki in Gicheon: Practices of Self-Cultivation in Contemporary Korea" (https://openaccess.leidenuniv.nl/handle/1887/50408).

There were many moments between 2015 and 2020 where we shared the ideas that have eventually coalesced into this book, including a panel at the Royal Geographical Society annual conference in 2014 with Victoria, Benoit Berthelier (now of the University of Sydney) and Wei-Cheng Lin of the University of North Carolina, Chapel Hill. I would like to remember panels at the eleventh World Congress of the International Association for the History of Religions, in Erfurt, Germany in August 2015 (with Victoria, the great David Mason and the extremely helpful Professor James Grayson), and at the 28th Academy of Korean Studies in Europe conference in Prague (with Victoria, David Mason, Nataliya Chesnokova and the esteemed Professor Keith Pratt) and a wonderful joint presentation between Victoria and myself at the Nordic NIAS Council Annual Conference in October 2014 at the University of Reykjavik, Iceland. Professor Tina Harris at the University of Amsterdam also supported us (as she has supported me on many occasions) in setting up an Asia Update event for us in 2016 at the University of Amsterdam. I very much want to thank Professor Mason for his work and guidance to us both and to myself. Equally I would like to thank Nataliya Chesnokova of the Russian State University for the Humanities, who completed work on her extraordinary thesis "Spatial Views and Self-Consciousness of Culture in Korea in the 18th Century. Based on the Historical and Geographical Writing 'T'aengniji' (1751) by Yi Chung-Hwan (1690–1756?)" in 2018 and who was a great if unexpected companion with whom to watch *SOLO: A Star Wars Story* in Moscow. I want to thank Professor Nianshen Song of the University of Maryland Baltimore County, whose brilliant book *Making Borders in Modern East Asia: The Tumen River Demarcation, 1881–1919* has helped me think a little less monolithically about Mt Paektu in recent years. The same is true of Professor Xiaoxuan Lu of the University of Hong Kong's School of Architecture, whom I met first sliding precariously down a mountain in Krygyzstan after the Asian Borderlands Research Network conference there in 2018. Together with her colleague Bo Wang, Professor Lu's visualisation of the complicated contemporary boundaries on and around Mt Paektu have travelled with me in the last years of this book's gestation. I want also to thank Professor Heonik Kwon of the University of Cambridge, who employed me as a Post-Doctoral Fellow at the beginning of this book's journey, and Professor Tessa Morris-Suzuki of Australian National University, who expected to see this book emerge while I was employed in Canberra, and whose book *To the Diamond Mountain: A Hundred Year Journey Through Korea and China* at least in part inspired this one. I will also thank the University of Leeds, which has had me as a Visiting Fellow during parts of this book's long journey, and Bath Spa University, whose Geography team will take the REF points for this in the 2021 evaluation process in the UK. Thanks also go to the anonymous peer reviewers for both Lexington Press and University of Hawai'i Press, whose guidance, critiques and suggestions have also helped shape the frame, words and structure of this book. As always I would like to thank Dr Adam Cathcart of the University of Leeds, who is always supportive of me and who has heard many times of the struggles to put this work together, and Professor Balazs Szalontai of Korea University, who has always been encouraging to me, but I imagine will enjoy this book less than my other recent work *Fish, Fishing and Community in North Korea and Neighbours* (still available Open Access via Springer, https:// link.springer.com/book/10.1007/978-981-15-0042-8). I again want to deeply thank Anastasia Artemova of the Russian State University for the Humanities for her wonderful design for my first book *Environment, Politics and Ideology in North Korea*, which has inspired the cover design for this book. Thanks to my initial editor at Lexington Press (Rowman and Littlefield), Brian Hill, and my later editor Eric Kuntzman, who were both extremely patient, so I am sorry to not be publishing this with you. I was so grateful to Lexington's support during early writing career. I am also as always grateful to Chris Reed at BBR, who has prepared, proofed and prepped this monograph. Finally, as always I would like to thank my partner, Hannah, for all her support, love and encouragement over the years (though she will be disappointed we couldn't make this book work in the way originally intended), and our little menagerie.

The research behind this book has been made possible through the generous support of the Academy of Korean Studies through the Beyond the Korean War project (University of Cambridge) (AKS-2010-DZZ-3104) and the Australian Research Council Laureate Fellowship programme (FL120100155). Elements of this book appeared as a journal article co-authored by myself and Victoria Ten ("New Goddesses at Mt Paektu: Two Contemporary Korean Myths", *S/N Korean Humanities* 2, no. 1: 151–79, https://www.snkh.org/Journal/ Article/22), and will appear as a chapter in *Invented Traditions in North and South Korea*, edited by Andrew Jackson, Codruta Sintionean, Remco Breuker and Cedarbough Saeji for the University of Hawai'i Press in 2021.

This book is dedicated to the many thousands of people across the globe who have lost their lives to Covid-19 in 2019/20, and to their families. We will all meet again, some sunny day.

## CHAPTER ONE

# Introduction

*New Goddess on Mount Paektu* is a book about transformations. It continues the exploration of the various manifestations of traditional East Asian goddesses carried out, for example, by T'ang (618–907) poets such as Chang Chiu-ling (Schafer 1980, 1).[1] However, in *New Goddess on Mount Paektu* the images of the goddess are transformed not by ancient poets but by the contemporary politics and ideology of North Korea.[2] I examine the processes by which ancient goddesses rise from archaic layers of culture and come into being and action in modern time and space. This 'new goddess on Mt Paektu' is constructed in present-day North Korea as a model, avatar and cypher for memory, projection and emulation. This goddess might look and dress differently, but the connections to older traditions are still visible. This is a mountain goddess, in the pages of this book intimately connected to the famous and powerful Mt Paektu, which has continued to increase in importance and conceptual stature in the present.

Considered an ancestral mountain during the Koryŏ (918–1392) and Chosŏn (1392–1910) dynasties, Mt Paektu gained further cultural and political currency in the Korea of the late eighteenth century (Kang, Sŏkhwa 2011), eventually becoming a symbol of the Korean nation in the twentieth century, as described in Chapter Two. The Korean peninsula is now divided into two sovereign bodies, split by a geographic and political rupture across its middle, far to the south of Mt Paektu. This division continues to be a source of intense pain and political

---

[1]  Shaman Mountain comes close to the sky,
A misted scene with a stretch of blue sparkle.
Here it was that the King of Ch'u dreamed,
Dreamed that he won the soul of the Divine Woman.

The Divine Woman has long since gone away;
Clouds and rain are gloomy, dark – and empty.
Here is only the wail of the monkeys of Pa –
No note of sorrow is to be heard.
      (Chang Chiu-ling, "Wu shan kao", CTC, 47, 565, referenced in Schafer 1980, 106)

[2]  Ideas which led to the composition of this book have been published previously in Winstanley-Chesters and Ten (2016).

destabilisation within East Asia. For a long time the political structures that have grown up on either side, far from working towards unification, were put to the use of contesting each other, each attempting to negate or nullify the authority of the other. Mt Paektu's geographic position is at the far northern border of the peninsula with China, since the 1960s for the most part within the territory of North Korea, a wilderness far from the centres of power. Given this, one might expect the mountain's place within the contemporary culture and history of the peninsula to be diminished. However, any visitor to either of the Korean nations will report the increasing importance of the Paektu landscape to both. The picture of Mt Paektu is present on the walls of North Korean political and institutional buildings, on billboards on the side of the COEX shopping mall in Gangnam, central Seoul, and on the mosaics at Seoul metro stations.[3]

Mt Paektu's slopes are complex, energetic, lively spaces that allow for the manifestation of new emerging mythologies that reconfigure and transform Korean cultural traditions. The hero of this book embodies the transformation from mortal into immortal in contemporary North Korean context, and represents the enmeshing of immortals with the social and natural landscape of Korea. Kim Jong Suk derives from the mythologies of North Korea and is reinvented and transformed by North Korean politics from child of peasant sharecroppers to guerrilla hero, revolutionary model and mother of the nation. Kim Jong Suk was the first wife of Kim Il Sung, founder of North Korea and its eternal Great Leader. She was the mother of Kim Jong Il, The Dear Leader, the nation's second figurehead, and the grandmother of Kim Jong Un, the current Supreme Leader of North Korea. To Kim Jong Suk I dedicate Chapters Three and Four of this book. Her image has not attracted much scholarly attention up to the present day.[4] In fact, this book is the first monograph in English in which she is the main protagonist. However, these pages approach Kim Jong Suk less as focal point or central narrative subject, but more as an example, an illustration of something else. The analysis of this book holds Kim Jong Suk and her story to be the reappearance in contemporary consciousness of an image of an ancient goddess as much as she is a political and guerrilla hero.

---

[3]   This idea was explored in an AKSE (Association for Korean Studies Europe) 2017 panel presentation, "Mt Paektu in North and South Korea – a Living Tradition".

[4]   Kim Jong Suk appears very briefly in a number of works on North Korea, North Korean politics, the Kim family dynasty and the notion of 'Paektusan Generals'. Dae-sook Suh's *Kim Il Sung: The North Korean Leader* (1995) has perhaps the most comprehensive recounting of her place within the family story. Morgan Clippinger's "Kim Chŏng-il in the North Korean Mass Media: A Study of Semi-Esoteric Communication" (1981) considers her transformation in North Korean media and publication, and Suzy Kim's "Mothers and Maidens: Gendered Formation of Revolutionary Heroes in North Korea" (2014) reviews the place of mothers and motherhood in North Korean mythology. Kim Jong Suk most frequently appears in the voluminous production of North Korean academia and historical publications.

Religious or spiritual practices embrace, interpret and utilise notions of gender, thus forming gender roles in a given society (Kendall 1987; Chong 2008; Han 2010; Han 2013; Han and Chun 2014). This book examines these processes in North Korea and raises questions of femininity, masculinity and gender around the processes of construction in such traditions. In contemporary feminist scholarship, gender is theorised as a complex set of practices, logics and institutions (Han and Chun 2014, 248). Suzy Kim identifies North Korean references to motherly love in the context of revolutionary discourse as radical selflessness in the interest of the collective (Kim 2014). As the narratives in this book clarify again, Kim Jong Suk is clearly represented as selfless, and selflessness is one of the main traits of her officially constructed image, as related in Chapters Three and Four. Yet, I suggest that the idea of motherhood in North Korean ideology stretches further than selflessness, for motherhood is one of the attributes of ancient goddesses. This book therefore attempts to identify elements of ancient connotations of divine femininity which resurface in contemporary times in new mythological forms. Kim Jong Suk, the 'new goddess on Mt Paektu', emerges in North Korea as a model, an avatar, a cypher for emulation and a feminine image, but applied across genders, inspiring – or attempting to inspire – women and men alike.[5]

North Korean mythology functions as a contemporary invented tradition, a term which echoes the famous study *The Invention of Tradition* by E. J. Hobsbawm and T. O. Ranger (1983). Invented traditions connect intimately with the concept of imagined communities developed by Benedict Anderson (1983). It is not by chance that these two monumental works, one on invented traditions, the other one on imagined communities, were published in the same year. Similarly to other communities, Korea was forced to imagine itself anew in the modern world and then reimagine itself again as two countries after the division of the nation. Because of this division, Koreans were compelled to imagine themselves as two separate communities, in opposition yet deeply related to each other. These processes thus produce new invented traditions. In their work on the form and process of North Korean politics, Heonik Kwon and Byung-ho Chung flag up in particular the invented traditions of North Korea (Kwon and Chung 2012, 63).

This book is certainly not a work of history or historiography in the pure sense. While I touch on historical themes as they are imagined in North Korea's new traditions, I do not claim that the narratives I encounter are authentically or coherently historical. This book does not study the sources as a historian might. I have chosen a limited selection of sources as my primary material, keeping

---

[5]   Suzy Kim talks about the feminine revolutionary models, particularly the model of devoted mother, which are applied across genders (Kim 2014, 261).

in mind that invented traditions invent also their sources, and those invented sources often utilise standard motifs in a number of ways. North Korea has produced a vast variety of different kinds of literature, extrapolating, extending or embellishing its core mythologies, and what it considers to be primary sources are few and far between. I do not limit myself to the analysis of North Korea's core narratives around Kim Jong Suk. I analyse the stories, but also the places where the narratives are set. I review how Mt Paektu itself functions in the legend of Kim Jong Suk, and how the landscape of the mountain impacts on North Korea's and individual authors' writing of the narrative. Both the writers behind the stories and the North Korean authorities already have a vision and understanding of the mountain in mind. This landscape exists in the collective mindset within particular political and spiritual cultures and the stories of Kim Jong Suk are deeply connected to Korean nationalism and spiritual power of Mt Paektu, seeking to do justice to the place as much as to the political ideology and ruling family generated from and by the landscape.

The study of invented tradition may seem slippery or too diffuse for the academic historian. However, any tradition is in a sense invented at some point, being an assemblage of the history and the myth-making, the real and the imagined. The traditions the goddess of this book represents certainly fit this model. The author of the book is a critical geographer with a focus on the intersection between topography and political culture in North Korea. After this book's agenda, key character, academic approach and sources are introduced, I review the theoretical frames applied in this investigation. The book is primarily focused on the transformation of this new goddess within the landscape of Mt Paektu. Therefore I primarily address work from Human Geography focused on the transformations of landscapes and mountain practices, including the approaches developed by Denis Cosgrove (2008), Noel Castree (2001), Erik Swyngedouw (1997), Jane Bennett (2010) and Sarah Whatmore (2005). This subset also includes traditions important for Korean mountain topographies and their place within the wider cultural matrix, as explained by David Mason (1999). I also include notions from self-transformation borrowed from Michel Foucault and the collaborative work with Victoria Ten that preceded this monograph.

## Mountain Practices

In the view of the author, mountainous topography is not a passive historical canvas for stories and invented traditions to unfold onto, but an active and energetic participant. This book relies upon the groundbreaking research of David Mason in his book *Spirit of the Mountains* (1999), one of the first works in English dedicated to Korean mountain gods. The ancient tradition of mountain gods described by Mason is a cultural source from which the frame for Kim Jong Suk as a goddess of the mountain emerges. *Sanshin* (山神, mountain gods and goddesses) are personifications of the spiritual and topographic power of the mountain.[6] These spiritual beings have complex and flexible relations with their local topography and the communities residing there. Spirits of some mountains were once humans entrusted with responsibility for particular mountain shrines, who have become absorbed into the landscape which they once served. *Sanshin* are male and female. It may be that some of the keepers and custodians of their terrain will one day themselves become *sanshin*. The *sanshin* tradition is therefore dynamic, active and generative, producing a landscape of divinities. This book examines the mythologies of a hero who I argue becomes a 'new goddess on Mt Paektu'.

The notion of the mountain as something potentially in motion, undergoing change, speaks to another key Korean tradition of *Paektu-taegan* (白頭大幹). *Paektu-taegan* is the mountain system of connected ranges that runs most of the length of the Korean peninsula, from Mt Paektu on the northern border with China down to Mt Chiri near the south coast. In Korean tradition *Paektu-taegan* is rather more than rock formations or tectonic outcomes. East Asian mountains, just like other things and beings in the universe, are considered to be the conduit for the transfer of *ki* (氣) energy, the life force. *Paektu-taegan* is a spine down which energy flows through the peninsula. The *ki* energy is then dispensed over the entire nation through various subranges. At the places where this energy manifests outwards, shrines and temples are established, which are often dedicated to *sanshin* (Mason 1999).

In this respect, the famous historical Korean work *T'aengniji* (擇里志) (1750?) by Yi Chung-hwan (李重煥 1690–1756?) is of critical importance.[7] It is a work of geographical synthesis rooted in *p'ungsu chiri sŏl* (風水地理說, theory on wind, water and land configuration), whose eighteenth-century author sought to connect these more ancient ideas of energy flow with developing rationalities and the social and material needs of an emerging Korean state. *T'aengniji* is described as the first work of Korean human geography and has

---

[6]  The author romanises this term as *sanshin* instead of *sansin* after consulting with David Mason. Professor Mason first introduced this concept in the English language a few decades ago romanised as *sanshin*, and accordingly the author of this book respects his right to define its spelling.

[7]  The original date of publication of *T'aengniji* is unclear. Yoon Inshil Choe (1996) suggests that Yi Chung-hwan wrote it between 1750 and 1751. It was first partially translated into English and published in 1998 by Wild Peony Press, Sydney. A complete translation has only recently been published by the University of Hawai'i Press (2019). Nataliya Chesnokova is currently working on the translation of *T'aengniji* into Russian.

been an important text for Korean topography, geography and nationalism (Chesnokova 2014).

*T'aengniji* and the ideas of *ki* flowing through the Korean peninsula might be considered to be a relational technology between ancient Korean tradition and the landscape. The mountains of *Paektu-taegan* serve as an example of the interaction between *ki* flow and the landscape that Koreans are familiar with. The relation between *ki* energy and the landscape connects to national identity in a way similar to the interconnections between personhood and life processes, like the mind and body of a nation. Yi Chung-hwan articulated a theory on the basis of which an authentic life lies in relation with the topography and landscape surrounding it: landscape influences the most auspicious place for living, what materials are required to build a house, and the availability of food. *T'aengniji* has been rewritten by more recent Korean authors, such as Cho'e Nam-sŏn, according to the needs and developments of Korean national sensibility (Chesnokova 2014); *Paektu-taegan* is transformed and reimagined in the present. These two key concepts support and underpin a complex web of other mountain practices and processes. Mountains are key players at the intersection of political and cultural narrative, they are participants in human history. Concepts such as *Paektu-taegan* and writings such as *T'aengniji* embed mountains in the cultural context of the Korean peninsula.

However, the notion of what constitutes a mountain itself is inherently slippery and diffuse, almost as much as the physical presence of a mountain appears monolithic and concrete. There is little consensus across cultures and historical periods as to what height or shape a mountain must be.[8] There are many examples of what Denis Cosgrove described as *High Places* (Cosgrove 2008) now brought low by time and cultural perception. Mountains and 'high places' can also be thought of through the other work of Cosgrove (1984) and scholars such as Noel Castree (2001) on the symbolic, social or political construction of nature and landscape. Following Henri Lefebvre's assertion that space and spatiality are themselves social and political products (1991), Cosgrove developed a conception of landscape and nature as symbolic, first through his analysis of the spatial organisation of Italian renaissance landscapes and later in studying the formation of the American West.[9] Castree viewed the function and utility of this symbolism in culture, politics and society with

---

[8]   Such as Scottish traditions of naming areas over 3000 feet a 'Munro' and those between 2,500 and 3,000 feet a 'Corbett'. When it comes to temporalities, summits in what is now the Republic of Ireland and elsewhere in Europe in medieval times, and in Australia prior to European colonisation, described as mountains or peaks are in the contemporary era seen as nothing of the sort.

[9]   In geography, space refers to the material landscape and topography, while spatiality indicates internal cultural relationships of individuals and communities with the landscape.

the eye of a critical geographer. Castree's analysis of landscape asserts that terrains and nature are themselves constructed by the societies and politics that inhabit them, marking them with symbolic power. Thus mountain places can construct political symbols and are themselves constructed by human ideologies. Erik Swyngedouw suggests that these constructed places become, through the processes of scale and scaling, "the embodiment of social relations of empowerment and disempowerment and the arena where they operate" (1997, 169). Swyngedouw understands scaling as the reimagining and rewriting of politics in different categories of social and cultural landscape. The notion of scaling has already been used to understand North Korean culture, but in this context it means that political ambition and agendas from one level of politics, the national or governmental level, are enacted at other levels. National-scale agendas are rescaled into the regional, county level, or the village or household private level. For example, every year North Korea has a tree-planting campaign directed at increasing the national level of forest cover, which embeds political ideas of productive and scientific forestry. At a local or regional level, party committees take the productive ideas of forestry and rescale them into smaller forestry projects, such as the beautification of parks. At the family or household level there are campaigns to grow fruit trees in private gardens. Families and private citizens thus rescale national agendas into their own living and personal spaces (Winstanley-Chesters 2015).

In studying natures and landscapes in this manner I further rely on the work of Jane Bennett (2010) and Sarah Whatmore (2005) on the generation of 'vibrant' or political matter. Bennett's work seeks to deconstruct the boundaries of human privilege over notions of agency through considering animals, plants, bacteria, viruses, metals and tectonic energy as actors in themselves, able to intervene or play roles in human politics. Instead of a politics controlled at the level of the human individual or human collective, these actors develop a distributed, inter- and hyper-personal politics which connects, contests and produces other forms of politics and agency (Bennett 2010). These active, vibrant materials and objects become political because of the role they play as stores of value, elements of exchange, items to be sought. In their exchange, seeking and obtaining they can transform political structures and infrastructures, be transformed by them and alter the cultural and social forms and landscapes in which humans live (Lorimer 2007). Notions of vibrant materiality and lively non-human actors can also connect to conceptions of political charisma, very active in North Korea. The energy and charisma of human politics are projected onto the trees in North Korean narratives and history. During the guerrilla struggles of Kim Jong Suk, for example, political slogans were carved onto the trees, and they thus become carriers of this political charisma. The trees become supportive in the narratives of struggle by providing places to hide, and by absorbing the shots of Japanese directed at the Korean independence fighters and activists (Anon. 2005; Nyŏjanggun 녀장군 2007).

As the author of this book developed his ideas of what landscapes, lively matters, 'mountain' and mountain practices are, he holds the work of Bernard Debarbieux and Gilles Rudaz (2015) in mind. Exploring the notion of mountain and mountain history, and examining the tensions in relations between culture, history and topography, Debarbieux and Rudaz speak not just to the topography itself, but also to the human and non-human dwellers of these spaces, the dwellers of the mountains. This is vitally important to this work focused on Mt Paektu where Kim Jong Suk exists in both chronological and cosmological time. The mountain becomes transformable by interaction with the process of mythological creation: North Korean monuments and memorials are erected on Mt Paektu, and infrastructures are built, contributing to and projecting state ideology and educational processes.

## Transformation and Technologies of the Self

Transformation of the character or the landscape is often made manifest by techniques, practices and strategies deployed by the characters within the text itself. 'Technologies of Self' has been a key concept for understanding the transformation of the protagonist in the narrative during the processes of this book's gestation and production. Michel Foucault (1926–84) examined the relationship between the ideas humans had about their own existence and the specific historical and cultural circumstances that shaped this existence. In recent years, connections have been drawn between Foucault and the philosophy of technology because Foucault also analysed concrete technologies used for exercising disciplinary power, such as the Panopticon (Foucault 1977; Dorrestijn 2012, 45, 47). In his later years, Foucault's interest shifted towards the technologies individuals apply upon themselves consciously and voluntarily. He talks about the technologies of self which:

> permit individuals to effect by their own means or with the help of others a certain number of operations on their own bodies and souls, thoughts, conduct, and way of being, so as to transform themselves in order to attain a certain state of happiness, purity, wisdom, perfection, or immortality. (Foucault et al. 1988, 18)

Foucault's earlier work constitutes the history of contemporary subjectivity – how we come to perceive ourselves today in particular ways, and what historical and cultural factors shaped our contemporary selves. His later work focuses on subjectivation – an active attempt by the subject to fashion and transform herself.

This later work investigates what kind of subject people wished to become in Greek Antiquity and the concrete practices utilised for this purpose. Foucault claims that the subject is not universally given, but emerges in the process of self-constitution (Dorrestijn 2012, 54, 58, 109). Constitution of the self occurs under the conditions applied upon the self by the outside world, but also follows a conscious will of the self. Examining the historical and social conditions that shaped our selves, and understanding the dynamics of self-formation which has already occurred, opens the way towards greater influence upon the future formation of the self in a given context. Foucault suggests reconsidering the history of philosophy from the standpoint of self-transformation (Dorrestijn 2012, 112). How did various philosophical doctrines shape the self? How were various philosophical doctrines the result of technological developments in a given era? How did people attempt to shape themselves and others through the use of doctrines and technical utensils? Not just the history of philosophy, but the history of humankind in general can be studied from the perspective of transformation of the self. This book therefore constitutes a case study of concrete technologies of the self applied in contemporary times in North Korea. The hero described is a paragon of perfection towards which ordinary people are expected, educated and instructed to aspire. The goddess, her images, and the stories and doctrines that stand behind them are also themselves instruments executing transformation in the readers or listeners of the legends surrounding her. The processes of this transformation are the subject of this study.

The concept of technologies of the self has multiple meanings. It includes the sense of 'practices of the self', but also of 'technical utensils'. In a way, any new invention of humanity constituted such a utensil: paper, ink-brush, TV and computer have all shaped our ways of being and our selves. Technical objects are directly connected to the practices of governing and fashioning oneself (Dorrestijn 2012, 109). The texts and images analysed in this book therefore constitute such technical utensils, employed throughout North Korean propaganda and its educational and pedagogic processes. Foucault draws connections between practices of self-transformation and the practices of truth: these practices require commitment, involvement and co-operation (Dorrestijn 2012, 113). This book discusses the various routes and techniques of production and construction surrounding North Korea's mythic reality. The mythic reality is revealed in texts, books, images and practices. This reality is not always perceived as complete truth, but there is no doubt that it still influences the mode of thought, feeling and action.

Michel Foucault's notion of technologies of self (Foucault et al. 1988) has been highly important for the author. Kim Jong Suk, the 'new goddess on

Mt Paektu', embodies the process of change, projecting the transformation further in space and time. This book asserts that, within the North Korean narratives of Kim Jong Suk, manifestations are found of similar techniques of self-transformation. In North Korea, technologies of self-violence and combative energy are deployed in the service of self-transformation: Kim Jong Suk and her followers passed through the process of change by acts of aggression and violence enacted by them and undertaken upon them. Violence in recent political history and theory has been best considered in the work of Hannah Arendt. Writing in the mid-twentieth century, "a century of violence", Arendt considered violence, including Bakunin's aggressive anarchism, Bolshevik urgencies and the chaos of the Khmer Rouge, as an "intoxicating spell" (1970, 67), dangerous and uncontrollable. In our present, political violence in its most dark and destructive form has become a common archetype to challenge the status quo of consumption and production. The transformative power of violence has a long history in politics, religion and the practices of self-perfection, allowing access to more powerful planes of knowledge, education and experience. Such dramatic transformations might seem to be in contrast to the subtle body practices described later in this book, but I suggest that these practices often include violent or dramatic events and narratives.

## Chapter Outline

Before giving an outline of the chapters, I will explain the logic behind the ordering of this book. The book explores the concept of transformation of the self, landscape and physical topography. The goddess of this book is transformed by her interaction with the physical terrain of Mt Paektu. Readers at some point in their lives will have walked up mountains. The heart quickens as one struggles up the slopes; the perspective expands at the summit; one feels relief and satisfaction upon having safely returned to the mountain foot from where the ascent began. The logic of this book mirrors or echoes the logic of a mountain ascent, hoping to transform the mind and body of the reader along the way. The book thus travels upwards through the foothills of context in this Introduction, bringing in Mt Paektu in Chapter Two. What is the meaning of Mt Paektu in the cultural context of the Korean peninsula? In Chapter Three the cultural terrain of mountain spirits in that land is studied. The North Korean ideology and historical narrative are discussed at the beginning of Chapter Four. Near the summit of the book, the stories of the goddess Kim Jong Suk are explored in Chapters Four and Five. In this transformative moment the readers reach the peak; the power of North Korea's mythology unfolds in front of their eyes. Then the reader begins the descent, down to Chapters Six and Seven and the Conclusion.

In Chapter Two, following the Introduction, the book delves into the cultural history of Mt Paektu. I examine the importance of Mt Paektu on the Korean peninsula and consider the evolution of Paektu as a modern tradition currently under construction. This chapter examines the literary productions which relate to the mountain, their connection with the history of the peninsula and the role of Tan'gun mythology for Mt Paektu. Then I investigate the projection of images of this sacred landscape into the everyday Korean present. The image of Mt Paektu is everywhere, from enormous mosaic reliefs on the walls of the Kim Il Sung mausoleum in the North to small vitrines containing plastic models of the mountain among the corridors of the Seoul metro system in the South.

Mt Paektu is vitally important for contemporary Korean culture. I suggest that this 'new goddess on Mt Paektu' from North Korean mythology can be considered as a contemporary immortal. In Chapter Three I consider how *sanshin* and mountain immortals manifest in contemporary Korea. Chapter Four focuses on the early years of Kim Jong Suk moving north across the dividing line at the 38th parallel. This chapter describes another moment of rupture in the history of Korea: the early years of Japanese colonialism. After the fall of the ancient governmental status quo of the Yi dynasty (1392–1910), Korean culture was challenged by the imperatives of colonial power from Tokyo. Much resistance to the new regime occurred within the boundaries of the colony, but much else occurred in the diaspora. Kim Jong Suk's family took an active part in an anti-colonial struggle, and the book engages with the North Korean historiography recounting Kim Jong Suk's early years, analysing how these narratives transform this young village girl into a revolutionary. A complex web of violence, politics and education in this story serves to reconfigure the young Kim Jong Suk, leading her to revelatory moments developing her political awareness; it further sets up her later importance to North Korean history.

Chapter Four starts with the difficult childhood of Kim Jong Suk, travelling with her to the landscapes of Mt Paektu. The crossing of rivers and wandering in charged landscapes takes her into the special transformative time, in the terrain of Mt Paektu. In a network of violence and topography Kim Jong Suk becomes almost superhuman, able to withstand intense pain, and subject herself to enormous deprivations. Proximity to the mountain serves to allow her transformation into an immortal. Kim's commemoration as an immortal in Pyongyang's Revolutionary Martyrs Cemetery today lies at a huge conceptual distance from her childhood in Hoeryong. Chapter Five thus leads the reader from the mythic space of Mt Paektu to the more contemporary terrains of North Korea today.

Chapter Six explores invented traditions in contemporary North Korea which connect with both Kim Jong Suk and other key characters in the charismatic political history of the nation. These newly invented and reconfigured traditions have been much in use in recent years, especially the School Children's March. In Chapter Seven I consider how the transformative possibilities function in mountain mythologies on the Korean peninsula. The previous chapters of the book delved deeply into the transformative power of the 'new goddess on Mt Paektu'; Chapter Seven considers other mountain practices in the West, mostly Europe, and in East Asia, mostly Korea and Japan. I outline the history and contemporary manifestation of social practices in mountain spaces, and touch on the landscapes of hiking in Korea and Japan. Finally I consider modern ascetics in Korea, particularly their efforts to contest new bureaucratic, economic and technological pressures in the upland spaces.

Chapter Eight constitutes a conclusion where I relate the results of the research within this book, within the dramatic landscapes, practices and persons the reader has encountered on the pages of this book. I hope that, with this outline in mind, readers can now satisfactorily engage with the narratives, becomings and transformations of this 'new goddess on Mt Paektu'.

## CHAPTER TWO

# Mount Paektu

## Introduction

As suggested in the Introduction, the North Korean political legends discussed within this book occur at Mt Paektu: a wild and charismatic terrain. For many years the mountain has been an important site of writing and research. The extensive analysis of English-language geographers and adventurers started at the turn of the nineteenth century (James 1888; Campbell 1892; Cavendish and Goold-Adams 1884). Having declined in the mid-twentieth century, English-language scholarship focused on Korean mountains and Mt Paektu has revived in more recent years with works that analyse mountainous spaces in fiction (Yu 1994), the place of mountains in agricultural and industrial production (Sorensen 1988) as well as mountainous spiritual spaces (Keum 1994; Mason 1999; Kim 2004; Shepherd 2010). For a number of contemporary scholars, such as Mason (1999), Park (2011), Ryu and Won (2013) and Dax (2015), significant subjects of interest included the hiking and tourist industries and the cultural space mountains occupy in Korean society in general. This book engages Korean mountains as a terrain within, through which contemporary mythologies are brought into being, brought into happening. Simultaneously, this mountainous background serves as the active, vibrant central image of the mythos itself: it feeds and creates its narratives, is constructed and recreated by and within them.

Mt Paektu is a fundamentally important cultural icon in contemporary Korea, both North and South. In North Korea's historiographies the mountain is postulated as vital to the struggle for independence from Japanese colonialism and as the birthplace of Kim Jong Il, its second leader; his signature is inscribed on the mountain in twenty-metre-high letters. In North Korean government and institutional offices, on one wall hang the portraits of Kim Il Sung and Kim Jong Il, while the opposite one almost inevitably holds a picture of Mt Paektu. We can see Mt Paektu on the front page of calendars printed in North Korea, while in South Korea murals and models featuring Mt Paektu decorate subway stations, including the Seoul City Hall station. Paintings of Mt Paektu are also frequently seen in South Korean governmental offices, in the lobbies of universities and buildings important to business and trade, as well as in less important restaurants and cafes. They are found in offices of some Buddhist temples, and in shrines dedicated to mountain gods. In both North and South Korea, Mt Paektu is often seen in photographs, and figures in poems, novels and films (Yi 2006, 35).

At first glance, North and South Korea appear radically different societies, possessed of opposing forms of government and economic structures. The first is an autocratic regime with a socialist past, the second is a hub of capitalism and global power focused on consumption. However, a deeper analysis of contemporary thought and daily practices of the two societies reveals the commonality of conceptual motifs. This commonality, originating in the cultural roots and shared past of a pre-divided Korea, actively unfolds in the present, taking embodied, actualised forms. This book explores the cultural, spiritual and political production that exemplifies this commonality of motif. The narratives of female power and action which are central to this book take place on Mt Paektu, a cultural stage co-produced in these narratives by the interaction and exchange between their participants. Therefore Mt Paektu requires a level of exploration, encounter and treatment within this book. This chapter gives a brief summary of the mountain's place in past and contemporary traditions as well as in the different streams of academic literature. I suggest that Mt Paektu is a living tradition currently under construction within Korean culture, becoming a symbol of both North and South Korea as Denis Cosgrove (1984) might have imagined. The mountain thus serves as exemplar of cultural, spiritual and political processes, connected to the narratives this book is centred around. Within offices and stations, shopping centres and important buildings, and in the media, images of the mountain appear daily to the eyes of citizens both in the North and the South. This chapter will explore the context for these images and their production, consider what recollections and emotions might be generated by them, and how the terrain of Mt Paektu might produce a fertile and welcoming space for these traditions and narratives.

## Mount Paektu History and Mythology

"Paektu San or White Head Mountain, lies seven or eight days journey to the west of Hoiryeng in Manchu territory. The mountain is in three tiers, is 200 li, or 60 miles, high, and the circuit of its base covers 1000 li, or 300 miles. On the summit there is a lake 800 li, or 250 miles, in circumference, whence flow the three rivers Yalu, Sungari and Tumen" – Making every allowance for the usual exaggeration in such matters, this notice clearly referred to a very uncommon sort of mountain! (Campbell 1892, 141).

Charles Campbell was one of the first European writers to encounter the topography of Mt Paektu. His journey has commonalities with a number of adventurers, travellers and opportunists whose journeys were enabled by the end of Korea's geopolitical isolation, the passing of a number of 'unequal treaties' and the pressing of colonialism on East Asia in the second half of the nineteenth century. In tandem with this reflection of Korean spiritual mountain traditions, the productions and mythologising discussed in this book echo some of the destructive, violent power of the Korean historical record, in ways that evoke the explosive tectonic past of Mt Paektu. Korea's history between the 1860s and the mid-twentieth century was certainly challenging and disrupting. The arrival of Western powers and economic interests in East Asia following the opening of the Japanese mainland with the General Sherman Incident of July 1866 and the June 1871 US campaign against forts at Kanghwa radically disturbed the status quo of Korean politics and social organisation under the Yi dynasty (1392–1910).[10] The Yi dynasty and the sovereign entity Chosŏn would not survive the interests of colonial and Western powers. The last years of the nineteenth and first years of the twentieth century were violent to the bureaucracies of the peninsula, generating radical reconfigurations of government institutions and transformations of social organisation, including the abolition of slavery and patterns of social hierarchy such as the Yangpan class as a result of the K'apo Reforms (갑오 개혁) of 1894–96.[11]

---

[10]  The General Sherman Incident of 1866 refers to an incident in July of that year when an armed merchant marine steamer, rented from the British company Meadows & Co. but under the command of a Captain Page of the US Navy, sought to visit Chosŏn (Korea) in order to negotiate trade relations. While much of the minutiae of the incident is disputed, what is not is that, not being invited or accepted, the *General Sherman* was attacked, ran aground, was destroyed by fire and the crew eventually killed. The Kanghwa Campaign of June–July 1871 was a more formal intervention, in part spurred by the events of 1866 and the General Sherman Incident, in which the US Navy sent 500 sailors and 100 marines on five warships to attack the Ganghwa citadel and five other forts nearby, killing nearly 250 Korean soldiers.

[11]  The K'apo Reforms (or Gapo Gaehyeok in Revised Romanisation) followed the chaos of the Tonghak Peasant Rebellion of 1894 and the Chinese and Japanese interventions of the First Sino–Japanese War. Between 1894 and 1896, under pressure from Japan, the government of

This was the nation encountered by Campbell, alongside others such as Isabella Bishop-Bird and Georgina Kemp, in the midst of radical change but full of cultural manifestations of more ancient traditions seldom seen or understood by outsiders' eyes. Campbell's report of his visit to the Korean peninsula to the Royal Geographical Society of London on his return in 1892 contains some intriguing descriptions of landscape and its cultural use. One analysis of his field reports suggests that at the outset of his travels Campbell focused on Mt Kŭmgang, and that Mt Paektu was for him something of an afterthought, which developed in importance as his journey continued (Jo 2009). However, Campbell's visit to Mt Paektu brought him into contact with a mountain which was conceptualised as an extraordinary hyperreal space, enormous in both geographical and cultural terms. While Mt Paektu is a very large mountain, it certainly is not 60 miles high or 300 miles across, nor is the summit lake, Lake Chon (천지, Ch'ŏnji), 250 miles in circumference. Given his invitation to talk at the renowned Royal Geographical Society, Campbell was not possessed of a tendency to exaggeration or overstatement, so what might possibly explain his conception of this mountain in such an enormous scale? Perhaps one reason for Mt Paektu's monolithic scale in Campbell's report can be found in those cultural, spiritual traditions which surrounded the mountain at that time and whose influence can still be found across the peninsula.

The legends and mythologies encountered on Mt Paektu within this book depict it as a place of struggle and of divine presence. In Mt Paektu's mythology, the divine presence is often feminine, manifested as adventures of the Goddess of Mt Paektu, or recounting the descent of heavenly maidens to the mountain's lake to play (Cho Hyun-soul 2010). Cho Hyun-soul (2010) also studies the historical development of Paektu mythology, and its reinterpretation in contemporary era for nationalistic purposes. Yi Yŏnghun (2006) considers new folkloric legends of Mt Paektu generated in the twentieth century and the development of Mt Paektu as a national symbol in the context of the reformulation of Korean history in the twentieth century. The vision of Korean history previous to the twentieth century centred on Neo-Confucianism and was part of the *sojunghwa sasang* (小中華思想, Korea as a small China world-view). Understanding Mt Paektu as being important to Korean tradition was part of this world-view, as evidenced from the travelogues of Korean intellectuals composed in the eighteenth century (Yi 2006, 25–8). In 1712, some of the landscape of Mt Paektu was incorporated into Chosŏn territory and the *Paektusan chŏnggyebi* (白頭山定界碑, Paektu mountain border marker), a

Chosŏn was required to reorganise its bureaucracy and government institutions, downgrade diplomatic and political relations with China, abolish the Yangpan and social class stratification system, reform the criminal justice system, abolish monopolies, liberalise trade policy and abolish slavery.

stone stele marking the border between Chosŏn and China, was established, so Koreans started visiting the mountain. However, special permission from the Chosŏn authorities was required for such visits, which were therefore rare (Pak 2013, 32).

This moment in 1712 can be conceptualised as a distinctly national event. Recent writing by Nianshen Song suggests that in 1712 Mt Paektu and its territory became rooted in supranational developments (Song 2018). Qing China had encountered new cartographic techniques, including the measurement of topography, through interaction with the Jesuits who came to China in the eighteenth century. The inclusion of Mt Paektu in Chosŏn territory in 1712 was a product of these interactions. Mukedeng, a Manchu official, with the permission of Emperor Kangxi, together with officials from Chosŏn, set out to use these new cartographic practices at Mt Paektu to counteract Russian claims on the area. Song recounts how, following a series of previous mapping mistakes, the hydrology of Mt Paektu was misunderstood and the boundaries drawn by the survey were thus incorrect. Song asserts that the Chosŏn officials in the surveying party were content to allow Mukedeng to place the border stele in a position that ceded the caldera and Lake Chon to China, and that this decision was taken in order to prevent populations of Korean settlers on the southern flank of the mountain, who should not have been settled there by past treaty with Qing China, from being seen by the Qing (Song 2018).

Pak Ch'ansŭng (2013) describes the process by which Mt Paektu came to prominence today as a symbol of Korean unification. He starts his discussion by noting the 2010 South Korean publication *Paektusan: hyŏnjae wa mirae rŭl marhanda* (백두산: 현재와 미래를 말한다, Mt Paektu: Speaking the Present and the Future), which is something of a landmark in the development of Mt Paektu as a living tradition of South Korea. As he summarises, the development of the image of Mt Paektu during the Koryŏ and Chosŏn dynasties was analysed by Song Yong-tŏk (2007) and Kang Sŏkhwa (2011), and in the end of the nineteenth and the beginning of the twentieth century by Andre Schmid (2007). Pak Ch'ansŭng himself focuses on the development of Mt Paektu as a national symbol in South Korea since the 1980s (2013, 11).

In 1908, the Korean nationalist historiographer and independence activist Sin Ch'ae-ho asserted that Mt T'aebaek, depicted in the *Samguk Yusa* (三國遺事, Memorabilia of the Three Kingdoms) as the birthplace of Tan'gun, the legendary founder of Kochosŏn, the first Korean kingdom, was not Mt Myohyang but Mt Paektu (Pak 2013, 23).

The foundation legend says that the god Hwanin's son, Hwanung, wished to descend from Heaven and live in the world of human beings. So Hwanin sent Hwanung to Mt T'aebaek, to settle there and to help human beings. The heavenly King Hwanung descended to a spot under a tree by the Holy Altar, on top of Mt T'aebaek, with three thousand followers. He called that place the City of God. Together with his ministers, Hwanung took charge of agriculture, allotted lifespans, illness, punishment and good and evil, and brought culture to his people. At that time a bear and a tiger who were living in the same cave prayed to Hwanung to transform them into human beings. The King gave them sacred mugworts and garlic, and instructed them to shun the sunlight for one hundred days. Both animals ate the spices and avoided the sun, but the tiger was unable to observe the taboo, and remained a tiger, while the bear became a woman. Unable to find a husband, she prayed under the altar tree for a child. Hwanung metamorphosed himself, lay with her and begot a son called Tan'gun.[12]

With the rise of Korean nationalism in the twentieth century, Tan'gun was reformulated as the father of all Korean people, rather than the founder of the first Korean state. The theory that Mt T'aebaek, the birthplace of Tan'gun, is actually Mt Paektu, and not Mt Myohyang, was very quickly spread by the Tan'gunkyo (檀君敎, Tan'gun religion) religious movement, which one year later changed its name to Taejongkyo (大倧敎).[13] In the 1920s and 1930s Korean newspapers started referring to Mt Paektu as *yŏngsan* (靈山, sacred mountain), reflecting and confirming its soaring significance in popular consciousness. Korean nationalists created and supported this new status of Mt Paektu in order to strengthen the spirit of the Korean nation in the struggle against the Japanese occupation. In his renowned *Paektusan Kŭnch'amgi* (白頭山 觀參記, Record on Visiting Mt Paektu), published in the newspaper *Donga Ilbo* (동아일보) in 1926 and released the following year as a separate book, the renowned nationalist Cho'e Nam-sŏn compares Mt Paektu to father and mother and describes it as wellspring of Eastern culture (Yi 2006, 28–9; Pak 2013, 26–9).

Following Korea's division in 1948, access to the mountain was blocked for southerners, but since the reopening up of China in the mid-1980s, South Korean citizens were again able to visit the Chinese side of Mt Paektu, and numbers of visitors from the South steadily increased. In the 1980s, South Korean newspapers started referring to Mt Paektu as to the "national sacred mountain" (*uri minjŏk ŭ yŏngsan in Paektusan, minjŏk ŭ yŏngsan*) (Pak 2013, 30). Being situated on the border between North Korea and China and reachable only through China, Mt Paektu came to represent in popular imagination not just the place where the Korean nation originated in the past, but

---

[12]   The Tan'gun legend is summarised on the basis of its translation in Lee and de Barry (1997, 5–6).

[13]   Tan'gunkyo (literally 'the religion of Tan'gun') is one of the new religions of Korea, originating at the beginning of the twentieth century and connected to the struggle for independence. The name was later changed into Taejongkyo, in order to obscure the nationalistic character of the religion during the Japanese occupation of Korea.

a symbol of the present division of Korea, giving at the same time a hope for future unification (Pak 2013, 31).

Nations require historical and semi-mythic narratives to underpin their political structure. Benedict Andersen understands this as imagined communities who create nation states in the Westphalian model (1983). These historical and mythic narratives require symbolic content from the community's past. In case of Korea these symbols include King Sejong, the Hangul alphabet, the turtle ships, General Yi Sunsin and, of course, Mt Paektu. The mountain is not alone as the only such symbolic peak in North Korea. Mt Kŭmgang, historically referred to as the 'diamond mountain' in Korea and now on the border between North and South Korea, is used as a landscape of national and personal unification over and above its traditional place in the nation's spiritual history, with its symbolic elements seeming to generate a new space in which emotional connections can be even briefly reforged and reconnected. Mt Chilbo, wholly within North Korea in North Hamgyong province and known as the home of a particularly powerful and tasty variety of mushrooms is, for Pyongyang, symbolic of places lost to South Korea by the nation's division. Fungus from Mt Chilbo has been strategically used in inter-Korean diplomacy and a bureaucratic tradition has developed around them at moments of connection between the institutions of the two Koreas. As such, these are examples of invented traditions utilised by imagined communities.

Mt Paektu and these other symbolic places have become a mountain anew in the sense Debarbieux and Rudaz (2015) would understand it. The glorification of Mt Paektu intensified during the second half of the twentieth century within the literary, artistic and cultural production of North Korea (Berthelier 2014) and various anthologies of Paektu legends were published (e.g. Chi 2004; Ch'oe 2006).[14] Even landscapes depicting Mt Paektu *without people at all* are used in North Korea to instil revolutionary sentiments in viewers and citizens, fulfilling the socialist role of art as 'educative' (Kim Il Sung 1964; Park 2011) and, for Park, signifying Mt Paektu as a newly invented tradition of North Korean art (2011). The popularity of Mt Paektu is rising for South Koreans as well, as evidenced by their frequent touristic pilgrimages to its Chinese side, and along the *Paektu-taegan* trail (Kendall 2009, 316; Mason 1999).

In considering the place of Mt Paektu in the contemporary cultural mythology of North Korea, this book follows the direction advocated by Koen de Ceuster in seeking to notice the different as well as the similar, and to take into account recent political and social contexts (de Ceuster 2013, 159). There is no doubt that the North Korean Kim Jong Suk legends came into being for the purposes of state consolidation of power and ideological education of the

---

[14]   I thank Benoit Berthelier for directing attention to these works.

people. I argue, however, that this does not undermine its creative impetus and its inherent connection with ancient Korean mountain tradition, which the Kim Jong Suk legend discussed in this book expands and continues.

Mt Paektu is often discussed in contemporary South Korean scholarship, a discussion that sets forth the significance of the mountain in the modern era. In contemporary times Mt Paektu connotes independence and rebellion motifs in both North and South Korea (Yi 2006, 31) but, in spite of the cultural or political importance of these stories, the current study does not aspire to provide a comprehensive review of Paektu-related culture in each of the two countries. Instead of a 'horizontal' coverage of Mt Paektu culture in different areas of life, such as literature, film, art, history, etc., this research is 'vertical': narrowing the scope to Paektu-related contemporary mythology only, the book therefore focuses on Kim Jong Suk's legends.

As a living tradition currently under construction, Mt Paektu became in a way a space of dialogue and communication between North and South Korea. South Korean scholars follow the production of North Korean contemporary Mt Paektu ethos with great attention, sometimes reflecting on it critically (Park 2011), sometimes constructing arguments similar in their contents to the Northern tradition. One example is the historical investigation by South Korean scholars of the Mt Paektu image as symbolic of the anti-Japanese struggle (Yi 2010, 113–18). Yet the contemporary Mt Paektu ethos is growing and developing on both sides of the 38th parallel, forming, in a way, one body of a contemporary tradition. The books discussing the mountain currently published in South and North Korea embody this contemporary tradition. One example is the previously mentioned *Paektusan: hyŏnjae wa mirae rŭl marhanda* (Mt Paektu: Speaking the Present and the Future), published in the South in 2010, which shows a similarity of narrative structure with *Mt Paektu Sacred to Revolution*, published in Pyongyang in 1989, and *Yet chidoro ponŭn Paektusan* (옛 지도로 보는 백두산, Mt Paektu Seen Through the Prism of Ancient Maps) published in North Korea in 2014. Northern and Southern texts rely on similar Korean historical sources, such as the *Samguk Yusa* and *Samguk Sagi* (三國史記, History of the Three Kingdoms), connect Mt Paektu to the origin myth of Tan'gun, and trace the significance of the mountain in Koguryŏ, Koryŏ and Chosŏn; both Northern and Southern sources mention that in Koryŏ in the twelfth century a deity referred to as Nation Protecting Paektu Mountain God was worshipped, enshrined as number one in the P'al sŏngdang (八聖堂, Shrine for Eight Saints).[15] Both *Paektusan: hyŏnje wa mirae rŭl marhanda* and *Mt Paektu Sacred to Revolution* abound with picturesque

---

[15]  P'al sŏngdang was dedicated to eight saints, each of them associated with a mountain god, a Daoist deity and a Buddha or a Bodhisattva. Hoguk Paektu Ak (護國白頭嶽, Nation Protecting Paektu Mountain God) was associated with T'aebaek Sŏnin (太白仙人, T'aebaek

views of the mountain's landscape, including of course Lake Chon, and describe the geography, climate, flora and fauna of Mt Paektu.

If the purpose of Cho'e Nam-sŏn and the other nationalists was to create and strengthen the image of Paektu as a cultural icon around which the people could unite (Yi 2006, 30), then their enterprise succeeded beyond their wildest expectations. Although these Korean nationalists could not and have not foreseen the division of the Korean nation into two different countries, their vision of Mt Paektu has greatly contributed to creating a connection point between North and South Korea, a symbol of so-hoped-for unification.

## Mount Paektu and Tan'gun Traditions in North Korea

How does Mt Paektu operate within contemporary North Korean tradition? How might historiographies of Tan'gun and the ancient Korean kingship function in the current North Korean context? This is a nation with a focus on the elimination of class difference, rejecting feudal practices. In the late 1940s and the 1950s, Pyongyang initially sought technical support and ideological inspiration from the Soviet Union (Cumings 1981), and Kim Il Sung's engagement of political, military and technical support deeply versed in Marxist analysis led to a rejection of past Korean historical or cultural traditions. The young North Korea was to be an intellectual space of materialist dialectics where a historiography of phases of development governed economics and controlled the modes of production (Cumings 1981). There was not a great deal of space within this framework for kings or kingship, especially not the mystical narratives of the Tan'gun or *sanshin*. The historical heroes of North Korea were to be the revolutionary guerrillas who had fought the Japanese alongside Kim Il Sung. They were reframed in the narrative to become historical foot soldiers and precursors to North Korean socialism through involvement in the Tonghak uprisings, the General Sherman Incident and the Righteous Armies of 1909–12 (Lim 2015).

Any reading of North Korean texts will generate an awareness in the reader that the content of these texts, including historical ones, can change and adapt over time. The importance of particular characters or events can rise and fall, others may appear and some may disappear. A good example from more contemporary history is the role of Kim Il Sung's mother, Kang Bang Sok, in presenting a useful female role model or archetype in North Korean literary and political culture (Kim 2013). Before the 1970s and 1980s, Kang

Saint) and Siltŏk Munsusari Posal (實德 文殊師利菩薩, Virtuous Munsusari Bodhisattva) (Cho Pŏp-chong 2010, 47; *Yet chidoro ponŭn Paektusan*, 232).

Bang Sok was a very important figure in North Korean history, eulogised by hagiographies of Kim Il Sung, events in her life forming part of institutional commemoration. As Kim Il Sung's son, Kim Jong Il, grew up to become the heir apparent to North Korean governance, the importance of Kang Bang Sok and the frequency with which her name would appear began to diminish, just as that of Kim Jong Suk, Kim Jong Il's mother, began to rise. In contemporary North Korea, Kim Jong Suk is a figure of extraordinary importance, allowing the transfer of a revolutionary sensibility from one generation to the next and providing a role model to the citizens (Winstanley-Chesters and Ten 2016). The transformation of Kim Jong Suk and her family into a revolutionary trinity and dynastic power at the heart of North Korean politics is offensive to orthodox Socialist or Marxist politics: there is no place for a mighty family who transmit power through a process of hereditary transition in a democracy of the proletariat, in control of the mode of production, free from superstition or feudal domination. Theoretically North Korea has sought to reconfigure its political structure through the adoption of a radical form of determinism ("Man is the master of all things") at the expense of Marxist materialist approaches. Yet historical precedent and historiography provided a deeper problem (Park 2012). It was necessary to build North Korea's authority and legitimacy on something more than nascent Korean nationalism, resistance to the Japanese and revolutionary commitment. The important history of Mt Paektu and Tan'gun was utilised for this purpose.

The mythology of the birth of Tan'gun and the emergence of Korean kingship and nationhood is deeply connected to Korean topography. The peninsula's mountainous geography related to the spiritual prehistory of the Korean nation includes specific mountains which play vital roles within the mythological narrative. The possibility that the birthplace of the mythical founder of the Korean nation, Tan'gun, came to be on Mt Paektu, now the sovereign territory of North Korea, could have proved difficult for Pyongyang's politics and ideology because the notions of Korean kingship, aristocracy and hierarchical social order contradict Marxist ideology. However, claiming connection to an authentic Korean national prehistory came to be vitally important for asserting North Korea's legitimacy. Tan'gun and the events leading up to his birth and the geography in which they occur are mythic, but they are currently considered not to pose a threat for North Korea's ideology. This mythography is especially important for North Korea's authenticity as a nation. The narratives of Tan'gun are distant in history yet they can be used in the production of effective and real geographies today. During the first decades of the North Korean regime the historical narrative did not mention Tan'gun at all (for example, the *Chosŏn T'ongsa* [Comprehensive History of Korea], published in 1977). However, in September 1993 North Korea announced its discovery of Tan'gun's tomb (Smith 2015), when archaeologists claimed to have extracted eighty-six bones from an ancient tomb, along with a crown and other royal accoutrements, supposed to belong to Tan'gun and his wife. Extraordinarily the bones were claimed to be some five thousand years old, pushing the existing historical narrative for the Korean nation some seven centuries back in time.

While Kim Il Sung, the 'Tan'gun' of North Korea would himself die the year after the discovery of the tomb, his son and grandson have made much of the melange of traditions surrounding prehistories of the North Korean nation. What this harnessing of ancient characters has done is allow a deeper frame for North Korea's history to be mined for authority and legitimacy by its politics. With the physical sites of Tan'gun's birth and death under its sovereignty, Pyongyang has been free to reconfigure its own political mythography, and commemorative architecture has been constructed on Mt Paektu within the framework provided by more ancient mythologies. According to recent interpretations, the power of the Tan'gun myth is rooted in the topography of Mt Paektu, which in turn is mobilised in contemporary times to support the revolutionary ideology of North Korea. Kim Chong-suk is one the symbols anchoring this ideology as Pyongyang repurposes the power of Tan'gun for the needs of its own political mythology and reprojects it back upon the topography of Mt Paektu.

## CHAPTER THREE

# Mountain Gods and Immortals[16]

The subject of this book is contemporary North Korean mythology which has common roots with the wider cultural and spiritual legacies of the Korean peninsula. The content of this common mythology is transformative processes in the mountains and the transfiguration of individuals from mortal into immortal, using a variety of techniques and processes. Mythological images of Kim Jong Suk from North Korea's powerful political legends grow from ancient East Asian cultures of immortality, and embody ideas of self-transformation, and furthermore instruct and inspire contemporary North Koreans to excel in self-perfection. The present chapter will outline the Korean cultural background from which these images and ideas spring. It will address notions of immortality and immortals and the development of these into alchemical practice, painting and religious cults. For the purpose of this study, it is important to distinguish between two kinds of immortal in the Korean context. The first are *sanshin* (山神), Korean mountain gods. The second are *sinsŏn* (神仙, Chinese: *shenxian*, divine immortals) or *sŏn* (仙, Chinese: *xian*, immortals). The discussion begins with *sinsŏn*, and *sanshin* are introduced in a later section of this chapter.

In East Asian culture, motifs of immortality, unending transmutations and reincarnations of life go as far back in history as national cultures themselves. The *sinsŏn*, an important figure in East Asian Daoism and practices of inner alchemy (內丹, Korean: *naedan*, Chinese: *neidan*) and nourishing life (養生, Korean: *yangsaeng*, Chinese: *yangsheng*), is a category within a hierarchy of celestial beings. *Sinsŏn* embody immortality, often a goal of these practices. Immortality, in this context, indicates a process of personal purification and enhanced perception of reality, resulting from physical, moral-spiritual and cognitive development (Kirkland 1991, 2008; Miura 2008a). Early descriptions of the immortals (仙, Korean *sŏn*, Chinese *xian*) are found in the Shiji (史記,

---

[16] I acknowledge Chapter Three as a work of co-production and inspiration between myself and my colleague and former co-author Victoria Ten (Jeonhwa Jeon). I am grateful for her inspiration and challenging intellectual engagement over the years. I would not have thought so much about East Asian immortals and mountain gods were it not for her.

Records of the Historian), produced around the first century BCE. Early East Asian immortals were sometimes depicted as clothed in feathers, potentially ascending to heaven by moving their arms like wings. Occasionally immortals took on the form of a bird, assumed a scaled body and a snake's head, with connection to mythic dragons. In East Asia dragons are renowned for being able to transform and change their form (Schafer 1980, 22; Miura 2008b, 1092). Images of dragons are thus widely utilised in alchemical texts, and in paintings the curves and twists of a dragon's body represent the endless flow and transmutation of life. These twists and curls represent the movement of *ki* (氣) energy, visualised in circles, spirals and waves.

## Sŏndo Culture in Contemporary Korea

While mountains and upland landscapes are vital for East Asian culture and spirituality in general, this is particularly true for Korean culture. Cults surrounding mountain gods (*sanshin*, 山神) have existed in Korea since ancient times. When Daoism came to Korea from China in the Three Kingdoms period, Chinese concepts of *sinsŏn* merged with the concepts of Korean *sanshin*. Today depictions of female and male *sanshin* and *sinsŏn* are found in shrines dedicated to mountain gods within Buddhist temple complexes, usually called *sanshingak* (山神閣) or *samsingak* (三神閣). They are also worshipped in separate shrines called *sanshindang* (山神堂), which are not part of Buddhist temples (Mason 1999, 97). Most *sanshin* are male, but there are also depictions of female *sanshin*, such as female *sanshin* images in Ssangkyesa (雙磎寺) and Daewŏnsa (大源寺) Buddhist temples at Mt Chiri (Chirisan). *Sinsŏn* are often painted on the outer walls of Buddhist temples, or as accompanying *sanshin*. *Sinsŏn* are sometimes called *pisŏn* (飛仙, flying immortals) or *sŏnnyŏ* (仙女, immortal women) (Mason 1999, 37–8, 55, 81). The term *sŏnin* (仙人, immortal person) can also be used.

The *sanshin* cult is alive in Korea in many forms: for example, Korean shamans pray to *sanshin* as they are included in a shamanic pantheon of gods and spirits, and separate ceremonies are widely held for *sanshin*. While *sanshin* is a very old and deeply rooted Korean folk culture, the *sinsŏn* tradition, usually identified as Daoist, was mostly favoured by the upper classes of Korean society, particularly during its introduction during the Paekche (16 BCE–660 CE) and Silla (57 BCE–935 CE) dynasties. In Koryŏ and Chosŏn, *sinsŏn* culture became gradually popularised, manifesting in such new religions as Ch'ŏndogyo (천도교) in the nineteenth century (Na 2012).[17]

---

[17]  Ch'ŏndogyo, or Chondoism, is a syncretic religion from Korea, deriving from the theologies and ideologies which drove Tonghak and the Tonghak movement. Son Pyŏng-hŭi reconfigured

In contemporary times, references to old Korean cults of mountain worship go under the name of *sŏndo* (仙道, the way of immortality). *Sŏndo* constitutes a merging of *sanshin* and *sinsŏn* cultures, embodied in the figure of Tan'gun. *Sŏndo* posits Tan'gun as central to *sŏndo*, despite the fact that the text of *Samguk Yusa* (三國遺事, Memorabilia of the Three Kingdoms) calls him *sanshin*, and not *sinsŏn*. *Sŏndo* culture has grown and developed since the 1980s, and it is postulated by its propagators to be an ancient and original Korean religion. New books on *sŏndo* are continuously published in South Korea, such as *Han'guk sŏndo wa hyŏndae tanhak* (한국 선도와 현대 단학) (Korean *Sŏndo* and Contemporary *Tanhak*) by Yi Sŭngho (2015), or *Han'guk sŏndo ŭi yŏksa wa munhwa* (History and culture of Korean *sŏndo*) by Sondŏ munhwa yŏn'guwŏn (Research Institute of *Sŏndo* Culture) published in 2006. These works perpetuate and develop the ideas of *sŏn* and *sinsŏn*, supporting their presence in the public consciousness.

Korean cults of mountain worship certainly have ancient origins, so the author of this book suggests that *sŏndo* can be defined as a newly invented name for an already existing cultural and historical phenomenon Alternatively, it can be argued that *sŏndo* is a newly invented tradition, which having grown out of ancient cults is taken up and developed in modernity. This reinvention of tradition can also be considered an act of rescaling, a geographical concept introduced in the Introduction to this book. This rescaling of the reinvented traditions impacts not only on the cults of mountain worship, but on the mountains themselves. The mountains as Debarbieux and Rudaz (2015) have considered are transformed by these traditions, and conceptually changed by these mountain cults. Old Korean cults of mountain worship are thus rescaled into the present, made legible, useful and functional. In its contemporary nationalistic meaning, *sŏndo* is a relatively new term. But the proponents of *sŏndo* in South Korea today project it backwards to Silla, Koguryŏ and Paekche (Sondŏ munhwa yŏnguwŏn 2006). They also view new Korean religions originating in the late nineteenth and early twentieth centuries, such as Ch'ŏndogyo, Chŭngsangyo[18] and Wŏn Buddhism,[19] as expressions of *sŏndo* (Na 2012).

---

and renamed the movement in 1905 ostensibly to make it more palatable to Japan and future Japanese administrators. The movement currently has over a million adherents in South Korea.

[18] Chŭngsangyo is one of a collection of new religious movements focused on spiritual renewal and the veneration of Kang Il-sun (1871–1909), a millenarian, messianic figure who combined elements of Taoism, Confucianism, Buddhism and traditional Korean shamanism.

[19] Wŏn Buddhism is a Korean branch of Buddhism emerging in the early to mid-twentieth century which sought to simplify, modernise and make more accessible the practices of Buddhism.

Korean cults of mountain worship were instrumental for the development of modern Korean nationalism at the end of the nineteenth and beginning of the twentieth century. When discussing the history of *sŏndo* as a term, its supporters point out its connection to what Sin Ch'ae-ho (申采浩, 1880–1936), Chŏng Inbo (鄭寅普, 1893–1950) and An Chaehong (安在鴻, 1891–1965) called *sŏn'gyŏ* (仙敎, the teaching of immortality). Hyŏn Sangyun (玄相允, 1893–?) called it *sindo* (神道, the way of spirits), Yi Nŭnghwa (李能和, 1869–1943) called it *singyŏ* (神敎, the teaching of spirits) and Ch'oe Nams-ŏn (崔南善, 1890–1957) called it *kosindo* (古神道, old way of spirits) (Na 2012, 411 n. 2).

*Sŏndo* culture is directly related to the cultural and social phenomenon of *chaeya sahak* (在野史學, oppositional history). The views of *chaeya sahak* are spread wide by its defenders, popular nationalist historians, and are accepted by many citizens of South Korea. *Chaeya* historians propagate the interpretation of Tan'gun myth which came up early in the twentieth century, when Tan'gun was redefined as the ancestor of the Korean people rather than the founder of the first Korean state. The conflict between the advocates of *chaeya sahak* found at the time outside academia, and the defenders of *kangdan sahak* (講壇史學, academic history), professional academic historians, escalated in 1978, focusing on the depictions of Tan'gun and Kojosŏn (古朝鮮) in school history textbooks. The proponents of *chaeya sahak* accused *kangdan sahak* scholars of promoting a colonial view of Korean history, instilled by Japanese scholars during the occupation. *Kangdan sahak* scholars called *chaeya sahak* followers non-professional and accused them of falsifying historical records. The main points of disagreement between the two groups relate to Tan'gun, the sphere of his operations in historical/mythological time and geographical space, and the reliability of various sources related to Tan'gun. *Chaeya sahak* see Tan'gun as a real historical figure, while *kangdan sahak* consider him a mythological character (Chŏng Kyŏnghŭi 2015, 155). Here again the power and authority of Tan'gun are rescaled from the past into the present, being utilised in a contemporary ideological debate.

Some contemporary scholars consider *chaeya sahak* to be new mythology, which attempts to strengthen Korean national identity, but Kang Tong-gu sees history and mythology as two sides of the same coin (2000). He notes that in recent decades the conflict between *chaeya sahak* and *kangdan sahak* has lost some of its acuteness, with some *chaeya sahak* claims being incorporated into the official version of Korean history, as demonstrated in contemporary history textbooks for schoolchildren (p. 14).

## Sanshin of Korea

The revival or reinvention of traditions of mountain immortality within the spiritual culture of Korea includes not only *sinsŏn*, but also *sanshin*. *Sanshin* are much more central to Korean culture than *sinsŏn*. *Sanshin* can be male or female, there can be one or more per mountain, they can be integral with it, and alternatively either manifest it or be manifested by it (Mason 1999, 34–7). *Sanshin* are usually described in legends as benevolent spirits. They help virtuous people and filial sons and daughters. *Sanshin* are also depicted as supporting historical figures and simple people in times of trouble, sometimes for no reason at all (Im and Pak 2005, 385).

The number and the size of *sanshin* paintings in South Korea has increased in recent decades and David Mason stresses that mountain worship is evolving new roles in twenty-first-century Korea (1999, 14–15), as evidenced by the growing body of research on the ancient and contemporary *sanshin* cults and practices. Korean academic scholarship discusses *sanshin* in the context of *sanshin sinang* (山神信仰, religious beliefs in mountain gods) and *sanshinje* (山神祭, festive sacrifice to mountain gods). A traditional *sanshinje* ceremony is performed in many Korean villages on a regular basis, in spring or autumn. *Sanshinje* is also performed in connection with burial, erecting a gravestone, hunting, and gathering ginseng on the mountain (Im and Pak 2005, 381).

Mountain worship became systematised under the Silla dynasty (57 BCE–935 CE). In his article on five mountains and Buddhist beliefs in mountain spirits, Ch'oe Chingu examines both the conflicts between *sanshin sinang* and Buddhism and their subsequent fusion. His article analyses Silla rituals of mountain worship described in both the *Samguk Sagi* (三國史記, History of the Three Kingdoms) and *Samguk Yusa* (Ch'oe 2013). Other South Korean scholars engage in historical analysis of the formation of *sanshin* mythology by examining, for example, the developments and changes in *sanshinje* ritual since the nineteenth century in Tonghaeri, Kongju. The orally transmitted legends explain this ritual as originating in sacrificial offerings to tigers in order to prevent them from attacking humans (Kang, Sŏngbok 2011). Similar research was conducted on the worship ceremonies for the mountain god of Mt T'aehwa (Pak 2009; Kang, Sŏngbok 2011), and the transformation of *sanshinje* in honour of the spirit of Mt Musŏng since the seventeenth century (Pak 2009).

In a number of further works, Korean scholars examine the deification of historical figures and their gradual transformation into *sanshin* (Yi 2000). An interesting example of this practice is the transformation of King Tanjong (端宗, 1452–55) into the *sanshin* of Mt T'aebaek. This process began in the fifteenth century, culminating in 1955 with the installation of a tablet at

Mt T'aebaek declaring a "memorial to the Great King Tanjong of T'aebaek mountain, Chosŏn kingdom". This happened in spite of King Tanjong having died and been buried elsewhere (Kim 2006). The cult of this former king and now contemporary god is popular in Yŏngwŏl county of Kangwŏn Province, and is examined in Korean academia as *Tanjong sinang* (端宗信仰, religious beliefs in Tanjong).

The examination of ancient and contemporary mountain worship in Korea includes the studies of the rites (Kim 2007), *sanshin* paintings (Kim 2005), and various types of *sanshin* legend and their structure (Kim 2003). One example is the study of the Mountain Goddess Tajagu Grandmother, worshipped in Chungnyŏng, Yongbuwŏn-ri, Taegang-myŏn and Tanyang-gun. According to the legend, this Goddess Grandmother defeated thieves operating on a mountain pass (Ch'oe 2004). Interestingly, Tajagu Grandmother and other mountain goddesses are often depicted as protecting the country during war or an uprising, and bringing victory. However, other legends feature the same mountain goddesses as supporting the enemy, thus causing defeat in a military conflict (Kwŏn 1998).

The relevance of *sanshin* for contemporary Korean society reaches beyond the ritual sphere of regular offerings to local deities. In Korea, mountains are traditionally regarded as a place where humans and gods meet, an idea accepted by adherents of different religions. For example, some Korean Christian researchers of *sanshin* suggest that a few pastors acquired spiritual powers through mountain prayer, and that these spiritual powers are expressed as leadership skills within the Christian community (Yi 1987). The *sanshin* tradition is thus rescaled into Christian practice: one example of how *sanshin* are deeply integrated with the landscapes, allowing for their legends to be reinvented again and again.

*Sanshin* worship today is connected to a number of contemporary projects, such as the Noksaek Han'guk (녹색 한국, Green Korea) environmental movement, and nation-branding (Mason 1999). These contemporary projects support the reimaging and reimagining of the mountainscapes again (Debarbieux and Rudaz 2015), as much as they revivify ideas of *sinsŏn*. The ideas of *sanshin* and *sinsŏn* are revived in the charismatic narrations and political mythology of North Korea, as discussed in Chapters Four and Five, and constitute a real element in contemporary Korean mountain culture and mythology.

North Korea's narratives focusing on Kim Jong Suk link these mythological concepts connected to the mountains to femininity. Scholars concur that the *sanshin* were held to be female in ancient times, and have mostly transformed, changing their gender to male under the prevailing patriarchal norms during the last half-millennium (Mason 1999, 37). Nevertheless, female mountain spirits are still actively worshipped in South Korea today, sustaining old traditions and evolving new ones. One example is Mt Unje, north-east of Kyŏngju. Today many female pilgrims frequent this Korean mountain to pray to the Unje Yŏsanshin (雲帝 女山神, Unje Mountain Goddess), the wife of Namhae, the second Silla king (Lee and de Bary, 51). Other examples of contemporary female-oriented Korean myths include the developing cult of "Mago, the Mother Goddess of the Korean people" advanced by adherents of the mind–body movement Dahn World. One of the most important female immortals in China, Mago (麻姑, Chinese: Magu) was allegedly born under Emperor Ming of the Han Dynasty (57–75 CE), and her cult in the regions of Anhui and Jiangsu had an active following until at least the thirteenth century (Despeux and Kohn 2003, 94–6). She became a mountain goddess from Korean folktales and is promoted in Dahn World mythology into a "mother of all humans", living in the "highest spot on the face of the earth" (Baker 2007, 511–13).[20] Another important female *sanshin* is Sŏndo Sŏngmo (仙桃聖母, Immortal Peaches Holy Mother), the goddess of Mt Sŏndo west of Kyŏngju. According to the legend recorded in *Samguk Yusa*, she gave birth to Pak Hyŏkkŏse (박혁거세), the first king of Silla. Later she become a promoter of Buddhism (Mason 1999, 38).

## East Asian Alchemy

Shifting and transmuting images of *sanshin*, *sinson* and their commemoration and veneration relate to another East Asian cultural phenomenon, namely alchemy. The purpose of alchemy is the achievement of immortality, which is considered possible after grasping the principles of life's origin and trans-formation. East Asian and European civilisations share "operational (external)" and "spiritual (internal)" alchemical practices and principles. European alchemical knowledge arises from ancient Greek and Arabic alchemy, which, there is evidence to suggest, developed under East Asian influences (Smith 2014, 126). Alchemical practices can also be considered through the lens of new materialism as articulated by Bennett (2010). In a view of the world based on Cartesian dualism the mind is considered active, the body is considered passive; humans are viewed as political, nature is viewed as acted upon. According to the theory of the new materialism, the material environment is vibrant and energetic; it has an independent agency. In alchemy metals and minerals are distinctly lively, they interact and transform. If the declared endeavour of external alchemy is the creation of an elixir that turns any metal into gold and gives eternal life, internal alchemy achieves perfection

[20]  See also Kwŏn (1998).

and immortality through transformative processes in the body and mind of adherents. In practice, external and internal alchemy often intersect and merge.

Ge Hong (283–343), an early Daoist thinker, discussed the art of immortality in his famous work *Baopuzi* (抱朴子, [Book of the] Master Who Embraces Simplicity), a core classic dedicated to internal and external alchemy. As he describes in the *Baopuzi*, meditation and purification have to be carried out before preparing the elixir. After the elixir is ready, gold is used to verify its perfection, and the elixir is proved to be effective when it can transform metals into gold; the perfected elixir which can turn metals into gold is ready to be absorbed by the seeker and it will turn a human into an immortal (Kim 2000, 145). Meditation and purification before the preparation of the elixir pertain to internal alchemy, while the process of testing the elixir on metals can be classified as external alchemy. Formulated this way, the process of preparation and absorption of the elixir of immortality manifests both internal and external alchemical processes, and the boundary between them is not clearly set.

The quest for immortality and the cult of immortals are rooted in East Asian culture and its indigenous religions. Immortality is achieved through the assimilation of that which is eternal, and is based on the life-ordering principle. There are different ideas of living immortality: to ascend to heaven alone or together with the family, to live long and secretly away from people in the mountains or at the sea, or to live among the people. In order to preserve life, one has to avoid sensory and psychophysical perturbations, so high position, power, responsibilities, glory and richness are considered obstacles for the path of immortality (Kim 2000, 23, 43, 48, 50). However, in certain historical periods pursuits of immortality were quite popular with the Chinese aristocracy, not contradicting but coexisting with high positions in society. The pavilions and halls of immortals in the mountains depicted in paintings often resemble an imperial palace, and immortals are dressed like high governmental officials (Munakata 1991, 130).

One of the routes towards immortality consisted in finding an immortal and obtaining from them a secret recipe for achieving immortality. During the Han dynasty the quest for immortality came to include not only finding an immortal, but also learning the discipline with the master in order to brew an immortality elixir (Kim 2000, 46–7). This quest for immortality was thus becoming a practice, a way of life.

Absorbing the elixir could grant the alchemist magical abilities, such as the wherewithall to summon the immortals, levitate and fly, avoid bad spirits, weapons or unhappiness, cure illnesses, regain youth, and – for older people – be able to bear children. Other potential abilities of an immortal included stopping epidemics, exorcising demons, avoiding poisonous snakes and resisting armed attacks. There are diverse methods of achieving immortality including virtuous actions, good conduct, ritual acts, medical, gymnastic and alchemic practices; Ge Hong emphasises the possibility of acquiring immortality through work and study (Kim 2000, 36, 48, 65).

In the practices of East Asian alchemy, nature includes atmospheric and astrological phenomena, as well as human life and social relations. For alchemists, nature manifests the practical application of life principles. Observing and imitating nature contributes to grasping these principles and creates an ability to apply them to one's own body. The purpose of alchemy is to transform substance, revealing and utilising its particular kind of energy. The means of the transmutation depend on the life force (*ki*) which is manifested and employed in a specific cosmic or organic space–time. The models of alchemic transmutation come from observing metamorphosis in nature, animal pregnancy, days and seasons of vegetal development and metabolism, as well as the transformation of minerals and metals (Kim 2000, 189, 193).

The time necessary for change in nature is too long for an alchemist, as for stones and metals maturation takes millions of years. But as the alchemist's human existence is limited, they attempt to accelerate the time necessary for the transformation of elements. This is a classic example of downscaling of the cosmic processes by replicating them in miniature. Both the alchemic melting pot in external alchemy, and the mind–body of the alchemist in internal alchemy, are conceived of as small models of the cosmos. These models unite time and space according to the function of the life principle, which is how they become a 'cosmic kitchen'. The time depends on maturation, the process of becoming. Becoming on the ground (planets and animals) and underground (minerals and metals) is stimulated and achieved by time, the sun cycles of day and night, summer and winter. Similarly, the transformation of the ingredients in the melting pot with the help of the flame, and formation of the elixir nourished and matured by the fire, has to be attuned to cosmic time. The duration of the heating and control of the fire are deliberately chosen and determined for their significance relative to the cosmic cycles (Kim 2000, 193–4, 209).

The elixir was composed of extracts of minerals, metals, vegetable and animal parts. Gold and cinnabar, representing permanence and transformation, often formed part of the elixir. First, it was observed that geologically gold can be found beneath cinnabar, and so the idea followed that cinnabar can transform into gold. Cinnabar was conceptually linked to the symbolic value of the colour red, associated with nobility, beauty and talent. In ancient China important documents were written in red, and red was a colour of the sun and fire (Kim 2000, 133–4, 141, 148). The Chinese character for cinnabar (丹, *dan*, Korean *tan*) means 'red colour', and *dan* became a generic term for an elixir of immortality (Kim 2000, 150). *Dan* forms part of the phrase 'cinnabar field', a term in internal alchemy which indicates three *dantian* (丹田, Korean *tanjŏn*), the three bodily loci which play a key role in East Asian practices of internal alchemy and nourishing life (Munakata 1991, 137). The three *tanjŏn* are located in the regions of the abdomen, heart and brain (Pregadio 2008, 302).

In alchemy, the evolution process of material is its refinement. In nature, time refines the material so, in the alchemic melting pot, refinement is the goal of alchemical operations (Kim 2000, 189–90). In internal alchemy, where the alchemic melting pot is the mind–body of an adherent, refinement, purification and harmonisation of the substances for creating the elixir translate into refinement, purification and harmonisation of the self, thus becoming – in the language of Michel Foucault – a technology of the self.

From an alchemical perspective reality itself is a chain of transformations. Alchemists attempt to discern the generative and productive principles of nature and create effects in their laboratories by employing the powers that reside in or derive from nature. In internal alchemy, the mind and body of the alchemist is just such a laboratory. The processes which occur in nature (macrocosm), alchemists try to imitate in the laboratory (microcosm), gaining and developing their knowledge of nature by replication and imitation. Imitation entails the ability to observe and reproduce, and observation and reproduction require self-reflection.

In this scheme, imitation itself acquires an epistemological status as the source of knowledge. Imitation is a productive activity, accompanied by beliefs and categories of thought that yield creation. The process of imitating nature itself constitutes a type of cognition (Smith 2002, 9–25, 121, 142). To imitate nature successfully, a bodily, experiential engagement with it is required. This engagement develops deep mastery of the behaviour of materials, such as that by which the carpenter knows how to choose, cut and prepare wood, and by which the miner knows his mine. This bodily involvement with the matter, which in East Asian cosmology is not dead, but alive and active, also shapes the body and mind of the alchemist (Smith 2002, 86, 98, 114, 117). In internal alchemy, the materials to be perceived and grasped are the 'self' of the adherent, continuously shaped and reshaped in alchemical process. Thus the work of achieving immortality is based on self-knowledge; it is a process where the self of the committed adherent constitutes material to be worked upon and with.

The work of achieving immortality is equally based on imitation of nature, which in the East Asian context is often understood as a mountain. The character *sŏn* (仙, immortality) consists of two elements, *in* (人, Chinese *ren*, human being) and *san* (山, Chinese *shan*, mountain) thus demonstrating direct connection between immortality and mountains in East Asian culture. Ge Hong stresses the importance of carrying out alchemic work in the vicinity of great mountains, and recommends for this purpose about thirty renowned peaks (Munakata 1991, 35). Contact with a mountain is therefore essential in internal and external alchemy: in the mountains immortals dwell; to sacred mountains seekers of immortality withdraw, where they seek herbs, minerals and mushrooms instrumental to alchemical processes. In internal alchemy a human body is often visualised in the form of a mountain (Despeux 1990, 194), and within East Asian paintings a mountain is depicted as a 'second self' of the adherent, and parallel processes and phenomena occur in a human body and in a mountain. This way painted images of a mountain, and subsequently a mountain itself, perceived and experienced by the committed following certain cultural 'programming', constitutes a model, or paradigm, of alchemic trans-mutation of the self (Kim 2000, 17–20), while the practice of painting becomes an alchemic practice of self-perfection.


## East Asian Paintings of Mountains

The culture of alchemy and immortality develops artistic representation as a technique of individual perfection and refinement. This culture has a long history: bronze ritual objects from the Warring States period (480–222 BCE), during the late Zhou dynasty, depict mountains as dangerous spaces of wilderness, where deities, monstrous creatures, animals, birds and sometimes humans engage in various activities, including hunting, fighting or dancing. Some bronze vessels portray the combatants pacifying or exorcising the mysterious realm naked, other than wearing crown-feather headgear. The dots marking the nipple areas suggest that they might be female. In some pictures, a winged human figure moves to heaven through a mystical realm of the sacred mountain. Kiyohiko Munakata proposes that this figure should be interpreted as a shaman on an ecstatic trip, a deceased person, or a spiritual messenger conveying the prayer of the people to heaven. In Munakata's opinion, these are early depictions of the immortals (Munakata 1991, 12–20).

Mountains as a dangerous realm of wilderness depicted in designs at the time of Warring States transform into more peaceful – or even festive – spaces during the Han dynasty (206 BCE–220 CE), where the immortals play music or dance in the mountains. During the late Han dynasty, individuals seeking immortality come to the mountains to engage in self-cultivation, to receive divine revelations, to attain magical powers or to prepare an elixir of immor-tality (Munakata 1991, 34), as reviewed in the previous section of this chapter.

One of the new iconographic elements in Han dynasty mountain scenes is the *yunki* (雲氣, Korean *un'gi*, *un* cloud, *ki* life energy) motif, sometimes called 'cloud scroll' in English. Its basic form is a rhythmic curvilinear pattern accentuated with cloud-like scroll forms that often suggest birds' heads or beaks and dragons' claws. This motif looks like a group of clouds charged with animistic energy. In the Han dynasty this cloud-like form becomes a vehicle of the immortals and these mystical curves serve as mountain peaks, cliffs, valleys, and bumps on a slope (Munakata 1991, 20–1). They are embodied in the depictions of phoenixes and dragons.

The art of depicting mountains developed during the successful era of the Six Dynasties (221–581). Scholars such as Gu Kaizhi (344–405) and Zong Bing (375–443) composed essays instructing how to draw a sacred mountain: this was to be drawn in the form of a writhing dragon, which expressed the ascending motion of a concentrated vital force (*ki*). In a picture, a narrow canyon with sheer cliff faces on both sides was suitable for the dwelling of the immortals. In addition, the painting usually included such symbolic elements as auspicious clouds, lone pine trees, vertical stone slabs, animals and birds (Munakata 1991, 36–41).

As already mentioned, a common alchemic motif in the paintings is a mountain which parallels a human body, and the first such representation dates to 1227 (Despeux 1990, 195). A later example is the picture known as *The Fanghu Isle of the Immortals*, Qing dynasty (1644–1911), in the Nelson-Atkins Museum of Art. Three palaces situated one above the other on a mountain can be interpreted as three *dantian*, while the mountain itself evokes the shape of a human body. Mountain paintings often depict people travelling towards the palace in the mountains, and these figures are also a metaphoric depiction of either *ki* or body fluids circulating through the organism. The complex symbolism of a mountain palace includes several interpretations, one of which is an imperial palace, and another a palace of mountain immortals. It can also represent the head of a human body.

A further example of a parallel between the human body and a mountain is a *Landscape with Buildings*, in the University of Michigan Museum of Arts (Munakata 1991, 134–5). On this painting the path leading to the palace curves just like intestines in the human body. The mountain itself is depicted as being dynamically in motion, transforming itself and transforming the viewer. The movement of people on the mountain is a multilayered complex metaphor, again connoting the movement of liquids and *ki* in a human body, the actual travel of people in a mountainous landscape, a pilgrimage to a sacred place, a journey to an imperial palace, and the spiritual progress of a human being towards immortality. Some of these processes occur simultaneously in old and new East Asian legends and images related to the quest for immortality. A moment of travel towards an imperial palace connotes a motif of improving one's status by ascending to higher ranks in the government bureaucracy and gaining social capital, an element which is definitely also present in immortality endeavours, as noted previously.

An argument in this book is that the symbolic images of the 'new goddess on Mt Paektu' represent a contemporary Korean immortal. These images inspire practices of self-transformation in North Korea intended to lead its citizens to think, feel and act in certain ways. Kim Jong Suk, the contemporary goddess, speaks to the ancient culture of immortality and alchemy of East Asia. Kim Jong Suk is an image directed at instilling revolutionary ideology in North Korea's citizens, and the way this goddess is depicted in contemporary North Korean texts and paintings follows the lines, motifs and techniques utilised in the traditional East Asian ethos of immortality. For example, the parallel between the human body and the mountain is one motif taken up and developed in the ideology of North Korea, and some political narratives sourced from Pyongyang even claim that Kim Jong Il, the son of Kim Jong Suk, resembles the famous Mt Paektu under which he was born according to the mythology of North Korea.

The metaphor of the mountain as a human body is important for practices of internal alchemy and East Asian medicine, where the human body is perceived as a system of *ki* passages or routes. *Ki* passes through acupuncture points which are vital for the life of the body, and the stimulation of these points can harmonise *ki* flow between the organs, heal illnesses and prolong life. These acupuncture points also connect *ki* from inside the body with *ki* outside the body, thus allowing the therapist to 'pump' new *ki* into the body of a patient. According to the parallel between the human body and the mountain, the process occurring in a human body occurs also in a mountain, and vice versa. Accordingly, acupuncture points in the human body parallel the places on a mountain where divine immortals ascend and descend.[21]

The parallel between a human body and a mountain relates to another alchemic model, not that of exposing the elixir to sun and heat as described in a previous section, but of placing it underground for maturation. In this model the alchemist recreates the space–time of the origin, of generation, where life germinates, reproduces and develops. This mechanism imitates the development of the embryo and the birth of a new life – conception and reproduction of life in nature – such that the genesis of the cosmos represented in the procedure parallels the gestation of a human (Kim 2002, 234). Here the earth, the well and the egg are the metaphoric images of the womb, and so the feminine body, within which an embryo develops, in turn becomes a metaphor for cosmos, for life gestation, and for an alchemical process (Schipper 1993).

---

[21] Kiyohiko Munakata provides a translation of a Tang source that notes the importance of the ascent and descent points of the immortals in the mountains, but he does not connect them to acupuncture points in the human body (1991, 2).

## Feminine Images of Divinity

Females are present in the arts of internal alchemy and life nourishment not only as abstract ideas and immortal deities, but as actual persons. Women have often taken an active part in Daoist cults: for example, in the Daoist school of Celestial Masters, which arose in the second century CE, women enjoyed a status equal to that of men. Women practised techniques similar to those studied by men and received similar titles, with leadership positions filled by members of both sexes (Despeux 1990, 19; Despeux and Kohn 2003, 105).

The Daoist immortal pantheon includes male and female figures and the cults of female immortals were particularly popular in southern China, with both male and female worshippers. These cults provided a space for active female participation which intensified in the eighth century when, as Daoism gained in popularity, it became fashionable for princesses of imperial blood to become Daoist nuns. Indeed, some of these cults included more female practitioners than male (Despeux 1990, 52). Feminine hagiographies popular at the time enumerated the techniques practised by famous women, which corresponded to those practised by men: abstention from cereals, internal alchemy, the recitation of canonic texts and the usage of talismans. These texts praised women for their achievements in painting, calligraphy, embroidery and poetry, demonstrating their spiritual perfection. Important abilities of perfected women included healing diseases and prophetic talent, and a number of important female Daoist leaders were famous for these; some were later deified and new cults were developed around them (Despeux 1990, 53–6).

Gary Snyder identifies "spirit of the valley" and "mother of ten thousand things" from the Dao De Jing (道德經), composed in the fourth century BCE, as echoes of a great goddess worshipped in Neolithic past (Snyder 1980, xiii). Edward Schafer calls her the "ancestress of all water goddesses of China" and compares her to goddesses of water and fertility from Babylonian, Greek and Egyptian cultures (1980, 42–3). In his book *The Divine Woman* he describes the development of feminine images of divinity in China focusing on the medieval period. Goddesses were also pictured as great creative powers of nature, but more often Chinese medieval poetry and prose focused on female immortals who came into contact with mortal men. This encounter was supposed to purify the body and soul of a man, and bring him incredibly long life. Over time, however, the erotic element of this encounter became increasingly explicit while the divine or purifying aspect diminished (Schafer 1980, 44, 46–7).

The motif of a romantic or sexual union between a mortal and an immortal comes from ancient times. *Chuci* (楚辭, Songs of the South), a collection of shamanic songs and ritual chants from the third century BCE, recalls that male and female shamans prayed for gods to enter with them into a close personal relationship. With prayers, fragrant flowers, dances and offerings the shamans enticed the gods to descend, and the meeting was accompanied by music and transmission of divine secrets (Despeux and Kohn 2003, 42).

The themes of physical love between a living person and a spirit appear everywhere in East Asian folklore and literature. Edward Schafer thinks that the fantastic journey of a male hero and his mystic union with a goddess is a motif that goes back to Babylonian times at least. By Tang times (618–907), a king or young scholar has replaced the archaic shaman in his meeting with the goddess. In Tang prose and poetry, an affair between a king/hero and a goddess takes place in a dream, or magic world, often on a mountain with a strong wind blowing, which in East Asian tradition is a symbol of *ki*. Attributes of the goddess are rain, mists, clouds and snow. Her "flesh and skin resemble ice and snow" and various mountain-related imagery is used to describe her; she is compared to stalactites, coagulated salts and magma. The goddess possesses alchemical secrets: here the motif of spiritual and physical regeneration is acted out through the agency of a divine sexual experience. The truth of her nature is impenetrable, she is difficult to attain, and sometimes the hero sees only her reflection in the mist, fragile and dreamlike, or hears only the echo of her song. In some stories the goddesses are described as cultivated ladies of the given epoch, but underneath they remain fierce and powerful, pitiless and lethal nature spirits that can deprive the hero of virility and drain him of his blood (Schafer 1980, 53, 93–4, 97–8, 101, 109, 114, 147–8, 188). Many of these motifs appear in North Korean contemporary mythology around Kim Jong Suk, who is transformed by the energies of internal and political alchemy to become something of an immortal, especially in the historiography of Pyongyang. In reality the invented and constructed mythologies around her draw on an immense cultural reservoir of East Asian mountain tradition and further develops it. It is to these stories and mythologies of Kim Jong Suk that this book now turns.

# Routes to Mount Paektu:
# The Young Kim Jong Suk

This chapter introduces the contemporary North Korean political goddess whose life is entwined with the extraordinary landscape of Mt Paektu. I briefly discussed Kim Jong Suk in Chapter Two but Chapter Four will focus on her early life. Before relating the biography of Kim Jong Suk, I briefly outline the history of North Korea's Kim family and their place in the political structure of North Korea. It is also important to explore some of the academic literatures which have been used to analyse the current situation in North Korea. The Kim family of North Korean rulers, designated in the national literature as the 'The Paektusan Generals', hold Mt Paektu very important to their history and political development (Berthelier 2014). The authority derived from the semi-mythical struggles against the forces of Imperial Japan in the vicinity of the mountain is projected onto the Kim family of rulers.

North Korean politics is regarded as an extraordinary, aberrant conceptual ideological landscape, layered with a multitude of theoretical approaches in academic analysis. Max Weber articulates the ritualisation of political action and intent used within institutional, governmental and bureaucratic structures in history and in contemporary times (Weber 1967), and his analysis has become a key to discussions on political landscapes characterised as authoritarian. Contemporary analysis of North Korean politics moves beyond Weber's theorisation: Heonik Kwon and Byung-ho Chung's landmark work *Beyond Charismatic Politics* (2012) brought an analysis of the theatricality of current North Korean political forms to the foreground, identifying what they termed the country's "theatric politics". Kwon and Chung's work made clear that North Korea's ideology allows its charismatic politics to spill out beyond the realm of conventional political interaction, marking and reconstructing both physical topography and text.[22] Continuing this line of thought I suggest that

---

[22] A key example is the reconfiguration of Pyongyang: Japanese colonial authorities had built modern Pyongyang following the tram lines from east to west. North Korea would later

all politics can be seen as theatre. Any theatre needs a stage, not just a debating chamber, but the physical topography of the nation on which political culture is written. Thus the landscape of the nation becomes a stage for the theatrical performance constituted by its politics. Kwon and Chung discuss the role of Kim Jong Suk in the formation of North Korea's theatric narrative around her (Kwon and Chung 2012, 58), asserting that in North Korean historical development Kim Jong Suk gained importance only when it became clear that Kim Jong Il, the son of Kim Jong Suk, was to be the heir to Kim Il Sung, the founder of North Korea. Of course, following Suzy Kim's development of the notion of revolutionary motherhood relevant for North Korean ideology manifested by the constructed memory of Kim Jong Suk (Kim 2014), this book concedes that the reality of this gendering is more complex and nuanced. In this book I therefore suggest that the stage for Kim Jong Suk's self-transformation extends further than her role as revolutionary mother, and that she in fact becomes a revolutionary archetype for all North Koreans to aspire to in the present, not just to revere in the past. Developing further Thongchai Winichakul's idea of geo-body (1994), Valenius (2004) has asserted that there is a close correspondence between the nation and the bodies of women.[23] In North Korean mythology the body of Kim Jong Suk is embedded into the landscape of Mt Paektu, becoming one with the revolutionary topography,[24] a revolutionary topography which has its own charisma.

I also suggest that in North Korea, charismatic politics necessarily beget charismatic landscape (Cosgrove 1984; Castree 2001). Charismatic landscapes such as Mt Everest, Mt Fuji and Mt Paektu are seen across the globe, with or without human interaction. When the threads and interactions of politics intersect with their physical terrains they become more than simply natural places. Occasionally landscapes in their meshing with social and political forces radically transform, and become places where ideologies themselves are reprojected by soil, rock and timber. Charismatic landscapes through the action of politics and ideology add to the conventional environmental realm, being denatured and at the same time renatured. Political charisma in the

---

reorganise the city urban planning on a north–south axis, connecting Kim Il Sung's birthplace at Mangyongdae with Kim Il Sung Square and the tower of the Juche (Joinau 2014).

[23]　The nation can be understood as constituted by the bodies of the people – the past, present and future inhabitants of the land. Thongchai Winichakul suggests that the landscape can also be considered as a body of a nation, and so the notion of geo-body suggests that landscape can be deeply entwined into the idea of nation itself (1994).

[24]　Some examples include cooking and camaraderie landscapes (places where Kim Jong Suk cooked and socialised with other female guerrilla fighters), and the romance landscape where her relationship with Kim Il Sung was acknowledged and confirmed (Winstanley-Chesters 2015).

landscape influences nature and environment, but at the same time produces and reproduces charismatic politics.

In this book, following Swyngedouw (1997), I suggest that in North Korea the image of Kim Jong Suk is rescaled across both space and time. When it comes to matters of space and spatiality, North Koreans re-enact her memory in national, regional and local campaigns, such as marches retracing the steps of Kim on Mt Paektu. When it comes to temporal matters, people today are encouraged to adopt her characteristics, such as physical strength and commitment to education in different areas of life: at work, school or home (Rodong Sinmun 2018a–g).

I have already mentioned the work of Kwon and Chung (2012) on political charisma and theatric politics in North Korea.[25] According to them, North Korean historiography and its present politics can be understood as an exercise at least in part of performance and theatre. The current North Korean politics derive power from the past through re-enactment of the past as real. However, this past is imagined and constructed in the present. This way charismatic political energy can flow forwards in time, adding legitimacy to historical or quasi-historical figures. In the Introduction I have already mentioned the rescaling of the authority of these figures, who introduce such charisma and theatric power into more conventional political events. In North Korea this process provides political energy and adds a useful fluidity to its current institutions. Focusing on the early life of Kim Jong Suk, Chapter Five will encounter the fluidity of North Korean political authority and charisma derived from history which creates narratives used to colour Kim's own life story. This reconstructed narrative is rewritten from time to time following changes in contemporary North Korean society and ideology.

Before I examine Kim Jong Suk's early life and the dubious historicity of her biographical narrative, however, it is important to give a brief outline of the circumstances that formed the background for her life. From the perspective of 2020 North Korea can be – and is – seen as a political outlier. In the past its conception of politics, history and culture could have been considered via the more common frame of anti-colonialism and liberation. North Korean historical narratives of struggle, overcoming and resistance to an overbearing colonial power were at one point very common across the globe. These narratives are replete with characters who serve as robust heroes of struggle and resistance, such as Kwame Nkrumah (of Ghana), Robert Mugabe (of Zimbabwe) and Nelson Mandela (of South Africa), who are famous in their nations as liberation heroes and national founders fighting for the achievement of either freedom or greater local equality (Birmingham 1988; Welz 2013).

---

[25]  The work of Kwon and Chung (2012) builds on that of Weber (1967) and Geertz (1980).

Given the contemporary politics and history of North Korea, it would now be difficult to conceive of Kim Il Sung or Kim Jong Suk within such a context. However, this is how their generation was originally imagined, and is how such stories were received by the forces of resistance and revolutionary politics in the wider world at the time (Young 2015), and the Korean peninsula itself was subjected to a form of colonialism which deeply marked its territory and from which its politics, culture or landscape have yet to fully recover.

In the nineteenth century the cultural and political status quo of Chosŏn, ruled by the Yi dynasty since 1392, was already under threat by social, economic and religious challenges, and being tested by the power and interests of Russia, France, the UK and an ambitious Japan (Duus 1998). After decades during which the Yi dynasty and social elite of Korea sought measures of reform which might allow the peninsula to be a sovereign place in a rapidly developing world, Korea was briefly made a protectorate of Japan before being annexed by the Empire of Japan on 29 August 1910.

Japan's annexation of the Korean peninsula was a comprehensive effort at colonisation. While Japan was happy to allow a vestige of the previous Korean royal house to continue in a reduced and constricted ceremonial capacity, the Government General of Chosen (the new name for the Korean peninsula), sought to reconfigure its political ecosystem (Caprio 2014). The Governor General (the first being Count Terauchi Masatake) built an infrastructure of power in which Japanese operatives and bureaucrats were highly important, deconstructing the patterns of traditional landownership which had supported the Chosŏn elite and inspired the social upheaval of the later Yi dynasty (Gragert 1994). The move by the Governor General's Land Survey Bureau to review patterns of land rights on the peninsula was at first popular, but it soon became clear that ownership would only be granted to those with formal written documentation. This excluded landholders and tenants of all classes, given the tendency for much of historical Korean land rights to revolve around oral traditions. Accordingly, Japanese settlers and private corporations (such as the Oriental Development Company) grasped control and ownership of much the land of the Korean peninsula; in 1932 a great percentage was owned by Japanese citizens (Gragert 1994).

Japan also sought to re-engineer Korean national and cultural consciousness later in the colonial period. There were a number of efforts by Japanese academic and educational institutions to systematise the understanding of Korean history and cultural production in strictly Japanese terms (Toby 1974), and new academic techniques of anthropology and archaeology were deployed to downplay some aspects of Korean history and to frame Korean cultural development in a particular way, supportive perhaps of Japan's efforts at "modernising" the peninsula (Pai 2000). When it came to the education system, at first the Government General of Chosen sought to institute what has been termed a 'hybrid' system, in which Korean language and culture were highlighted – using newly developed models of history from Japanese research institutions – as backward and inferior (Toby 1974). At the same time Japanese was taught as a vital, modern, international language, and the history of Japan was taught with a particular focus on the Japanese Empire as set out in the context of the Imperial Rescript on Education (Toby 1974). Towards the end of the colonial period, as the Japanese Empire developed its military capacity and prepared for war in the Pacific, the pretence at hybridity was abandoned, and Korean language teaching was abolished in the public sector and then banned in private institutions (Toby 1974). Under the policies of the Government General of Chosen, Koreans in the late 1930s and 1940s were to accept what has been termed 'Imperial subjectivity' through the *Nissen Ittai* concept.[26]

This later period of Japanese colonisation after 1933 would see the industrial and economic infrastructures of the Korean peninsula put to urgent work at the behest of Japanese militarism, thus becoming a vital resource base for the pursuit of Japanese industrial and military development (Caprio 2014). This reconfiguration of the land echoed earlier elements of the colonial project in which agriculture and forestry had been brought under the principles of Japanese science and industry, and the landscape itself made more Japanese in nature by planting Japanese trees (Fedman 2015). At the time Korean conceptions may have varied from the optimistic to the hostile, but the product of Japan's colonial exercise has most often been Korean resentment and hostility.[27]

During the colonial period numerous independence movements had differing approaches to the struggle against the Japanese, with varying degrees of success. The initial annexation in 1910 led to several years of struggle between the Japanese on one side, with the vestiges of the Yi Confucian scholarly bureaucracy and the remains of the *yangban* elite class, known as the Righteous Armies (Em 2013), on the other side. Later, following the death of Emperor Kojong in 1919, the March 1st Movement sparked a year or more of anti-Japanese resistance and spurred the foundation of the Provisional Government of the Republic of Korea in Shanghai (Em 2013). After 1919, resistance against the forces of Japan moved away from the terrain of Korea or Chosen itself. Korean democratic nationalists would find

---

26  Nissen Ittai (日鮮一体, Korea and Japan are One) was a Japanese social and institutional project in colonial Korea during the 1930s designed to dissolve the differences between notions of Korean and Japanese nationalism. This was achieved through a focus on Japanese language and reducing the influence of Korean, as well as focusing on Japanese history rather than Korean. This was, however, not instituted on the Japanese mainland where the distinctions were still encouraged (Shin 2014).

27  A number of Korean intellectuals welcomed colonisation by the Japanese Empire as the route to Koreans' interaction with the brave new world of the modern (Poole 2014).

homes around the globe, advocating national refoundation from a number of different cities and institutions (Lee 1984). For this book, guerrilla movements are particularly important: in North Korean historiography they are presented as having developed in the borderlands of the north of the peninsula and in Manchuria. Advocates of Korean independence settled in these areas, supported by funding from the Soviet Union and international communist movements. Japanese documents record that the guerrillas that harassed the Japanese forces on the border between Korea and Manchuria did on occasion mount an attack close to the areas near to Mt Paektu (Haruki 1992). Later, through the process of narrative reconstruction by North Korea, this struggle was reimagined closer to the mountain, as Mt Paektu grew in importance to North Korean cultural mythologies. In reality much of this struggle occurred further to the north. When considering this reconstruction, it is important that North Korea and its political elite are in many ways a newly imagined community (as Benedict Anderson articulated in 1983), just like Koreans at the time of the colonial period. During the period of Japanese dominance, Koreans were encouraged to reimagine themselves and their community according to frameworks and concepts not their own; Nationalist Koreans or later North Koreans would imagine their community anew using newly invented traditions (Hobsbawm and Ranger 1983) which were rooted in these reconfigured mythologies.

Within the invented tradition of North Korea, Kim Jong Suk is one of the advocates for Korean independence, and she is imagined by North Korean history to have become deeply engaged in the series of battles near Mt Paektu. While she belonged to the disparate band of followers around Kim Il Sung, in the narratives of North Korea these guerrillas are depicted not only as fighters against Japanese Imperial power, but also as inheritors of other histories of Korean national struggle: Kim Il Sung's relatives are recorded by North Korean historiography as having been involved in the General Sherman Incident, the Tonghak Uprisings of the 1880s and with the Righteous Armies of 1910–12 (Lee 1984). Whatever the veracity of these accounts, they are connected by a similar thread, thus providing a suitable canvas to which other narrative elements can be added. Mythologies and mythographies of North Korea are built round these narratives involving a vast number of actors, both material and immaterial, sentient and non-sentient, divine and non-divine (Doty 2000). For the most part these mythographies occur in mountainous and wilderness places in the north of North Korea, in particular Mt Paektu, and involve various actors, such as mountains, rocks and animals, which are transformed by human culture and politics (Debarbieux and Rudaz 2015). The present chapter considers one historical character from such a mythography of Mt Paektu, imagined in North Korea as a focus of revolutionary activity.

## The Revolutionary Childhood of Kim Jong Suk

The mythology generated by the hopes, dreams and aspirations of Korean nationalist resistance sits within the cultural and social contexts of the years in which it was created. Kim Jong Suk's childhood life and activities for the most part occurred away from Mt Paektu, in the area of the Soviet Union, but through acts of historical reconstruction and imagination have been *post facto* sited at Mt Paektu. She was born on 24 December 1917 in colonial-era Korea, and at the age of four fled with her family to Manchuria. As such Kim Jong Suk has a very human prehistory, a real childhood and a life similar to that of her husband Kim Il Sung. However, the reality of her childhood is in a sense lost within the constructions of North Korean narratives, so I consider the processes by which the image of her as an immortal is created. First, this chapter attends to her prehistory as it is presented by North Korean historiography with all its imagination and mythology. Then I examine the content generated by North Korean historians and political writers in order to deliver a back story which would underpin her later transformation. This back story itself constitutes an invented tradition (Hobsbawm and Ranger 1983).

Kim Jong Suk's revolutionary prehistory begins with her childhood, itself a product of the Japanese colonial period and the Korean diaspora of the 1910s and 1920s (Anon. 2005, 9; Nyŏjanggun 2007, 1, 4) and in many senses familiar from other writings and memoirs. However, the cultural and social processes that make up her childhood were developed earlier. Kim Jong Suk's history is far less extensive than that of her husband, Kim Il Sung, and her son, Kim Jong Il, whose hagiographies are as detailed as they are disputed by external observers. The texts that describe her are less voluminous in size and less frequent in number. North Korean historians have gone into intricate and obsessive detail to locate Kim Il Sung at particular moments of his life, sometimes with some success. Kim Jong Suk, however, has not been subjected to quite the same forensic or archaeological historical review, in spite of becoming an important figure within the North Korean revolutionary pantheon revised during the 1980s (Lankov 2007). Elements of her life story tied directly into the narratives of her husband are addressed within works by Dae-sook Suh (1995), Bruce Cumings (1981) and Sydney Seiler (1994), to name just a few commentators from the wider academic world. But the primary texts describing Kim Jong Suk's life are indigenous North Korean publications with their attendant problems of veracity for academics and readers.

As previously mentioned, I do not assert that these publications hold to acceptable levels of historicity or truthfulness. On the other hand, I also do not accept the assertions that this renders them useless to critical or academic work (Myers 2011), particularly not when it comes to the examination of legendary or historical female characters bestowed with magical powers and their interactions with Korean topography, the themes this book deals with. I primarily use the anonymous biography published in the English language by Pyongyang's Social Sciences Publishing House and Foreign Languages Publishing House in 2005 to navigate the life of Kim Jong Suk. The Korean-language version of this biography is known as 녀장군 (Nyŏjanggun). I have used both the English and Korean versions of this biography, though the text and the order of events in these two versions can be substantially different. I also refer to the later English-language biography *Kim Jong Suk Anti-Japanese Guerrilla Heroine* (1997), as well as the three volumes of *Reminiscences (With the Century)* (1993–2007), published in Korean in 1992 as 세기와 더불어 (Segi wa tŏburŏ), apparently by Kim Il Sung as autobiography.[28] There are also extensive bodies of other material on Kim Jong Suk generated by North Korea over the decades. In addition, numerous paintings and graphic representations of Kim Jong Suk demonstrate elements of her character and history visually. There are poems and songs about her, some of which are still sung today as part of North Korean musical repertoire (Rodong Sinmun 2018h), and there are even theatre and opera pieces about Kim Jong Suk and her female guerrilla band (North Korean Leadership Watch 2017). Finally she is remembered in the architectural and institutional fabric of the country through the naming of places such as the Kim Jong Suk Textile Mill (Rodong Sinmun 2018i). These various manifestations of Kim Jong Suk's mythology are part of a wide network of different materials and memorial places, inform the textual elements I use primarily in this book, and constitute vital parts of the invented tradition surrounding Kim Jong Suk.

Within the body of literature and hagiography, Kim Jong Suk's constructed story shares some commonalities of theme and content with that of Kim Il Sung. This is true in relation to the description of an early period in her life. Kim Jong Suk is presented as having been born of peasant parents, father Kim Ch'unsan and mother O Ssi, at Osandong village,[29] Hoeryong County, on 24 December 1917 (Anon. 2005, 9; Nyŏjanggun 2007, 1, 4). Within the narrative, Kim Jong Suk's parents encountered Japanese colonisation in its

---

[28] Kim Jong Suk's *Biography* was published in 2005 by the Social Sciences Publishing House and Foreign Languages Publishing House in Pyongyang. 녀장군 (Nyŏjanggun), the current Korean-language version, was first published in 2007. There is a 2017 version available online. *Kim Jong Suk Anti-Japanese Guerrilla Heroine* was published in 1997 by the Foreign Languages Publishing House, Pyongyang. *Reminiscences (With the Century)* is published in English by the Foreign Languages Publishing House, Pyongyang, and in Korean by the Workers Party Publishing House, Pyongyang.

[29] The English text of the *Biography* says that the family comes from a small village in Hoeryong called Osandong, The Korean text of Nyŏjanggun does not mention the name of the village and refers only to Hoeryong.

harshest, most degrading form, similarly to the parents of her husband, Kim Il Sung. The text suggests they had always been subjected to ill-usage of a sort. "Her family had moved from place to place, being mistreated and exploited by landowners" (Anon. 2005, 9; Nyŏjanggun 2007, 3). Kim Jong Suk's family in this text includes her mother, father, two elder brothers and one younger brother. Kim Jong Suk's parents and grandparents, similarly to those of Kim Il Sung, had been controversial and politically active characters. Though the campaign is not stated by name, we learn that "Her grandfather had participated in a peasant uprising against Korea's feudal rulers", which is a reference to the Tonghak uprisings of the late 1890s. Following the death of the grandfather in 1908, her family "became worse off, under the burden of increasing debts" (Anon. 2005, 9; Nyŏjanggun 2007, 3–4). These burdensome debts were incurred not simply due to the inequitable impositions of landowners: "Her father, the pillar of the family, was frequently away from home working for the independence movement" (Anon. 2005, 9; Nyŏjanggun 2007, 3–4).

The commitment of Kim Jong Suk's father to the cause of Korean independence and his resistance against Japanese imperialist power brought them familial disruption and financial difficulty. "The family, unable to pay back its debits, lost its share of cropping land and its thatched cottage was pulled down. They had to live in a room in another family's house on Osan Hill" (Anon. 2005, 9; Nyŏjanggun 2007, 3–4).

Aside from the financial impact on Kim Jong Suk's family, there is an acute and determined violence within her early history. Kim Jong Suk's father died in "a foreign land" in 1929, her mother who "helped her husband in his patriotic struggle" was killed "by Japanese 'punitive' troops in 1932", and her elder brothers were both killed fighting the Japanese as part of Kim Il Sung's forces (Anon. 2005, 7). The coagulation of violence and death within one revolutionary family is similar to the family of Kim Il Sung.

The violence is tied to other elements of her development, used by the narrative in a transformative way. The reader will see how Kim Jong Suk's personality evolves through educative experience, revolutionary political awareness and military training. These practices would support her social and political growth, allowing her to become a better, more capable individual, to gain control over a challenging life. Kim Jong Suk harnesses the power of her own development as a Foucauldian technology of self (Foucault et al. 1988). For North Koreans interested in the hagiography of their historical leaders, awareness of Kim Jong Suk's story becomes itself a technology of self, necessary for the instigation of their own ideological maturity. The themes of violence, perseverance, survival and overcoming, just like the difficulties of her family, are vital elements of Kim Jong Suk's transformation, technologies through which this transformation happens in the text.

Violence is utilised by Kim Jong Suk, her fellow actors and the narrative writers in both destructive and constructive ways. Destructive violence manifests when fellow guerrillas are being brutalised and degraded within the narratives, affecting the readers in particular ways. The constructive influence of such violence is demonstrated when Kim Jong Suk harnesses violent impulses to overcome her own body and self, depriving herself of food and sleep in acts of self-cultivation, a classic example of applied technologies of self. This feeds back into the processes of transformation and becoming, leading to further overcomings.

Another important narrative device and textual motif in the transformation of Kim Jong Suk is the 'crossing of rivers'. River crossings in North Korea's historical narratives are vital moments of transition and self-transformation. The Tuman and the Amnok rivers are key sites of crossing for Kim Il Sung in North Korean revolutionary mythology.[30] Kim Jong Suk also appears to have shared with her husband a tendency for intense remembrance of moments of river crossing. The North Korean tradition amplifies the burden of colonial oppression on the individual: once Koreans cross the rivers at the boundary of colonial Chosen they feel freed from the oppression and subjugation of Imperial power. In world mythology the crossing of a river can also be an important moment of transformation of the self.[31] Crossing the rivers therefore activates the mythological power within the historical narratives, generating transformative possibilities for the characters in them. Kim Il Sung's crossing of the Tuman river in 1918 serves as the moment of political awakening in his narrative: having crossed the river, Kim Il Sung operates in a different space, free from the bounds of colonial politics. Now he is able to develop his own political sensibilities and eventually to act on them for revolutionary purposes. Kim Il Sung is transformed in this space; the future of the revolutionary movement which he would lead and which gives birth to North Korea is also transformed. Here the crossing is a technological element of the narrative; it acts not only upon the person crossing the river, but on the landscape itself. The crossing is transformative as for Kim Il Sung so for the supposed readers of the story, forming their way of thought and feelings in a given direction.

Kim Jong Suk also crosses a river early in her life, later conceiving of her own crossing of the Amnok as a vital moment in her upbringing and development. The crossing of this river is itself a technological aspect of self-improvement within the narrative. The crossing is transformative; it embeds a geographic locality in her consciousness connecting it to nationalistic aspirations:

---

[30]  The River Tuman romanised in McCune–Reischauer is often referred to as the River Tumen in academic writing.

[31]  In ancient Greek mythology, crossing the River Styx signifies a passage from the world of living to the world of dead; in Buddhism crossing the sea of *samsara* brings an adept to the island of *nirvana*.

I never lost the memory of my hometown after I left it. At every moment of joy or sorrow, fighting under the General's command, I thought of my hometown Hoeryong. When on a march or in battle, I felt a little easier, but whenever I looked up at the moon shining on the camp in the forest, the trees, grass and pebbles of Hoeryong swam before my eyes. (Anon. 2005, 10; Nyŏjanggun 2007, p. 5)

In this sense geography and nationalism are connected for Kim Jong Suk. In her later years this connection is embodied in Mt Paektu, for according to the contemporary version of the Tan'gun myth, when the god Hwanung descended to Mt Paektu, characters both mythic and historical can be reborn and transformed there.

The North Korean authorities reconfigured the personality of Kim Jong Suk in the texts, utilising objects from her childhood[32] and places from the later revolutionary period of her life.[33] These locations are used to reimagine Kim Jong Suk's personality as that of a revolutionary fighter, just as the moments from her childhood are deployed in order to embed particular behavioural or emotional tropes within her narrative construction. We will see later that a form of revolutionary fraternalism is a key personality trait embedded within the texts recounting her life. This trait is demonstrated in a narrative addressing her early years, when her *Biography* recounts that "from her childhood, Kim Jong Suk gave thought more to the welfare of her parents and brothers, and her neighbours than to herself" (Anon. 2005, 10). This selflessness takes many forms within the text. Having accidentally broken one of her mother's earthenware jars (described as "part of her dowry", therefore culturally important), the young Kim Jong Suk attempts to make good her accidental damage. She gains employment at a kiln which pays in earthenware jars. This would seem an honourable and ethical thing to do, but her decency is amplified further. When refused a job at the kiln on account of her age, before turning disappointed for home, "she saw that one of the women working there had a crying baby on her back. Feeling pity for the woman, she took the baby from its mother and cared for it until noon" (Anon. 2005, 10).

Another episode of Kim Jong Suk's sacrifice, related to her family's difficult situation in quite dramatic and revealing terms, describes how she was compelled to collect edible herbs for her family. On her way home:

---

[32] Hoeryong, the town in North Hamgyong Province where Kim Jong Suk was born, is home to the Museum of Revolutionary Accomplishments of Kim Jong Suk. The museum has a collection of Kim Jong Suk artefacts such as her walking sticks, wedding ring, school uniform, first pistol, etc.

[33] These places include areas where Kim Jong Suk made camp and cooked on Mt Paektu, Lake Samjiyon, and birch trees under which her relationship with Kim Il Sung was confirmed and commemorated. Many such places became memorials and museums.

she heard the crying of a baby from a hut at the foot of the hill. It sounded so pitiable that she entered the hut, to find a young woman ill in bed with her crying baby sucking at her breasts that had run dry. (Anon. 2005, 11)

Such a desperate situation does not phase the young Kim Jong Suk. Instead she is recounted as having "lifted the baby onto her back and, lulling it to sleep, cooked gruel with her herbs, and served it to the woman […] before returning home with an empty basket" (Anon. 2005, 11).

## Kim Jong Suk's Education in Nationalism

Kim Jong Suk's *Biography* spares none of the misery of her childhood years, making sure to recount all the possible unfortunate instances which befell her family: "In their new place, their standard of living went from bad to worse. Her father was laid up with illness, her crippled elder brother was unable to work properly, and her sister-in-law was suffering from a disease after childhood" (Anon. 2005, 11). Would it really be surprising if anyone subjected to such difficulty developed a combative or restive streak? As Kim Jong Suk grows older the feminine characteristics involving care (such as cooking, hygiene or personal grooming), are scaled and rescaled within the political and historical narrative through its foregrounding of her connection to North Korean combative nationalism. These practices of care marked by selflessness that began in her childhood are later amplified to include the entire Korean nation, and in this way the reader of the narrative is encouraged to perceive that how Kim Jong Suk cared for her siblings and family as a child is the way she later cares for the whole nation.

The importance of Korean education and language during the colonial period has been the subject of intense academic analysis in Korean and Japanese studies (Caprio 2014). Running counter to Japanese efforts to transform Koreans into imperial subjects under the *Kokutai* principle (Caprio 2014), the inculcation, continuation and survival of local linguistics and culture was regarded by the colonial authorities as an intensely political act (Poole 2014). It was important for the colonial authorities to directly engage the Korean community in the exercise of becoming a new imagined community, and to forget or unimagine their previous historical reality. Accordingly, in the later colonial period, Korean-language education and publishing were eradicated and made illegal (Caprio 2014). Maintaining the Korean language was as difficult within the diaspora as it was at the periphery, so although Kim Jong Suk's family were not resident in the colony itself, the restrictions also applied to them. Kim Jong Suk is presented as having been an eager pupil: "she herself wished to learn. The stronger her desire to learn, the more bitter was the resentment she felt at the heartless world which denied her a decent life and an opportunity of learning" (Anon. 2005, 12). In this sense her education is itself a technology of self, utilised both for her own transformation and development, and for later deployment in revolutionary activity as a weapon of nationalism. As she moved from childhood to adulthood, the resistive nature of Kim Jong Suk finds an initial home and is later amplified by her educational technologies. Pedagogical interactions provide the opportunity to establish connections between her and the political group which would later eulogise her and in which she would find fulfilment, family, death and memorialisation.

Pedagogical development and educative practice have vital importance and cultural tension in revolutionary politics over the world. Revolutionary theorisation has usually been an exercise of the very few or the elite. For example, the famous anarchist theorists Pyotr Kropotkin and Mikhail Bakunin were both born of the Russian aristocracy: Kropotkin was actually a prince of the Rurik dynasty of Tsars who ruled before the Romanovs, with family possessions of some 1,200 serfs. The British socialist William Morris was raised in a wealthy family of London financiers; the father of Karl Marx was from a line of rabbis and a successful lawyer in Prussian Trier. Revolutionary politics as it is known in communism or socialism has sought to escape this elitism and to harness the power of a small group of committed activists. Therefore, a key practical strategy for the revolutionary elite to gain power was to break out from the small group of theoreticians by spreading education among the masses. This is clear in the historiography of the Bolshevik uprising that overthrew Tsarist and Social Democratic power to form the Soviet Union in 1917. Bolshevik historiographers, for instance, record as 'agitators' those who were vital participants in inculcating Marxist or Leninist theory among the working class; their support would be essential in enabling the Russian revolution to succeed and persevere (David-Fox 1997). Over time particular figures from non-elite groups, such as Alexey Stakhanov in the Soviet Union or the whole population of the agricultural village of Dazhai in the People's Republic of China, would become fundamental to the processes of workers' agitation or education (Shapiro 2001). These exceptional personas would serve as models to follow for other workers and non-elite groups, exemplars of both personal behaviour and political practice, and stories about such models would become part of revolutionary education (Shapiro 2001). In a sense the bodies and energies of these exceptional personas were deployed as technologies of the self within the political structure.

There are a number of examples of revolutionary movements in which one generation of the educated are cast aside by revolutionary practice as being beholden to counter-revolutionary or old-fashioned beliefs. A particular case is that of Cambodia following the revolution which brought Pol Pot and the Khmer Rouge to power and formed the Democratic People's Republic of Kampuchea for three brief yet bloody years. Pol Pot had theorised that his revolution brought 'year zero' to Cambodian society, a detemporalised state of being where there was no past and no history, only the present and the future (Bergin 2009). Intellectuals of the past were perceived as a threat to the new regime, so they were neutralised and executed whenever possible: history records that Pol Pot's regime killed teachers, lecturers and intellectuals, even to the extent that it sought the death of those who wore glasses, as a signifier of intelligence (Bergin 2009). While this looks like an entirely anti-intellectual or philistine regime, the Khmer Rouge had in fact extensive theories on educative practice (Bergin 2009). Having created a blank intellectual slate through killing, the Khmer reformulated the mental world-view of the population through the education of children. The regime would use these newly educated revolutionary children to re-educate and to keep in intellectual check their parents and older members of society (Clayton 1998). These children were themselves technologies of self deployed by the Khmer Rouge bureaucracy to transform other citizens. However, education was not the only technology at their disposal, for the Khmer Rouge sought to use the cathartic and brutal process of bloodletting and death to generate intellectual epiphanies in those exposed to its revolutionary cause (Bergin 2009). While Pol Pot and his followers did not have long enough to instigate the entirety of their pedagogic revolution, the transformative power of these technologies of violence and education has been deeply important to many of the more esoteric revolutionary movements of the late twentieth century.

Both the more urgent moments of Maoism during the Great Leap Forward and movements later influenced by Maoism, such as Peru's Shining Path and India's Naxalites, would privilege the transformative technological power of violence and education (Gorriti 2000; Chakravati 2009). One could access an authentic, activated revolutionary nature by abandoning the ignorant, pre-revolutionary self through acts of violence and education. This way the new revolutionaries would become opposed to their past lives and unlikely to return to previous ways of being. The reader will see many of these processes and practices in the education of Kim Jong Suk. For the revolutionaries seeking to overthrow the forces of the Japanese Empire and instil their own particular Korean national subjectivity, both violence and pedagogical practices were key technologies in the process by which young Koreans were enticed or encouraged to join the movement.

Kim Jong Suk's desire for education was fulfilled when a Korean language school was founded in the village where her family lived. This way North Korean historiography connects her educational experience with a key vector of Korean nationalism, the bettering of Korean language skills.[34] As she had to work and to care for her family, Kim Jong Suk attended the school at night. She was taught by Kwak Chan-yong who "was engaged in anti-Japanese patriotic enlightenment as a member of the revolutionary organization formed by the young communists dispatched by Kim Il Sung" (Anon. 2005, 12).

Kim Jong Suk's first educational encounter is presented as a dramatic epiphany:

> How grateful I was at the news that the night school had been opened! […] that was the first gratitude I had felt in my life, I was so happy that I shed tears holding onto the edge of the blackboard. (Anon. 2005, 13)

The world of revolutionary nationalism now opening up to her had an intense physical impact on her person: "back at home that night, Kim Jong Suk could not sleep". Kim Jong Suk's emotional educational experience bridges the narrative gap between her childhood and adulthood. It connects the lack of agency in the prehistory of her family to active political future and the later transformation of Kim Jong Suk within the landscape of the North Korean revolution. The most dramatic elements of this process occur in the mid-1930s, her education providing the initial vector for this transformation.

"Comrade Kim Jong Suk looked much more developed than her age in those days. She was clever and well behaved and eager to learn." This quotation from the recollections of Rim Chun-chi (an "anti-Japanese revolutionary veteran") portrays Kim Jong Suk on the cusp of her becoming an adult. She was exposed to new paradigms of political conception and social relation, "the fact that there were kind people who were sympathetic to the poor in the cruel world excited her personally" (Anon. 2005, 13). The realisation of inequity and exploitation within the diasporic and colonial Korean society spurred her on to continue her own education and support others in accessing such new knowledge:

> She advised her friends who were hesitant to come to the school, saying that women too should learn how to read and write so that they could see clearly the injustices in society and get rid of outdated feudal ideas. (Anon. 2005, 13)

Kim Jong Suk's early steps in education began the process of transformation to be subsumed into revolutionary struggle. As is often the case in the narrative of her life history, this struggle is presented as a combination of education and the social relations in her family and community: "in those days, Kim Ki-jun

---

[34] The preservation of the Korean language was an important priority for Korean nationalists and has become mythologised in contemporary Korean culture, for example in the 2019 South Korean film, 말모이 (Mal-Mo-E: The Secret Mission).

was a hardcore member of the AIU [Anti-Imperialist Union]. His family did not know this, but Kim Jong Suk sensed that her elder brother was working by night for a great cause" (Anon. 2005, 14). Developing a sense of nationalism and social oppression, she resolved to become more deeply involved with the revolutionary movement. The movement was eager to support her in political transformation; her night school teacher was even supported by the Young Communist League to better train Kim Jong Suk for revolutionary ends. Naturally for North Korea's historiography, it was Kim Il Sung's revolution she "believed would win back the lost country for the nation, provide the Korean people with a new world free from exploitation and oppression, destroy the Japanese marauders and put right the evils of society" (Anon. 2005, 15).

Kim Jong Suk's first revolutionary act naturally brings together her familial, educational and political connections:

> One spring day in 1931 Kim Jong Suk turned up at a rendezvous at the foot of Mt Nan [...] From a shady thicket her night-school teacher appeared. Some distance away, Kim Ki-jun was standing. Her heart throbbed with a feeling of respect for her brother and pride in having such a brother. (Anon. 2005, 15)

This first act of concrete rebellion was leafleting in the village; one leaflet "was even pasted on the gate of the landowner's house". This way Kim Jong Suk attempted to entice in her fellow villagers a protest against exploitation, a form of political technology utilised to promote the transformation of the self in other people. It seems that during the middle of 1931 Kim Jong Suk was busy learning, engaging in agitation and underground work. The text focuses distinctly on the utility of her youth and gender for tactics of struggle: "To avoid the enemy's watchful eyes, she disguised herself as a peasant girl going to sell edible herbs, like a girl going to school, or as if she and her younger brother were going to visit relatives" (Anon. 2005, 16).

In this chapter the reader has seen the development of Kim Jong Suk within North Korean historiography, from her birth as a peasant in Hoeryong to the beginning of her transformation into a committed revolutionary. So far this transformation is described as having been spurred by external and internal factors. The external factors include being impacted by economic structure, deprivation and persecution by the state – in short, suppression of the whole family by the wider capitalist system. The internal factors include her desire for education, to overcome the Japanese, and to seek retribution on the people who hurt her family. Her familial misfortune and cruel treatment by the colonialists and landlords, typical for North Korean narratives, serve as a precursor to the violence meted out by her and wrought upon her as described in the next chapter. Equally her belated access to education, while developing her sense of nationalism and subjectivity as a Korean, would take Kim Jong Suk to the precipice of transformation. Kim Jong Suk's subjectivity would be radically converted by the process of pedagogical interaction, particularly through the use of affective techniques. Kim Jong Suk's own agency would become vital for the processes of change and resistive encounter. The next chapter will show how Kim Jong Suk, as human actor within a historical mythography, was encompassed by an active landscape which effects and affects change. Kim Jong Suk will move into the landscape she called home in her early youth and this is where she concludes her transformation. Within the North Korean narratives recording her life and death, the personality of Kim Il Sung becomes a key element in these new spaces. It is clear that Kim Il Sung is the centre of the political movement during this era, with all others orbiting around him in some way. From this centre emanates an energy which draws those interested in the potential transformation of Korean politics and political subjectivity towards Kim Il Sung himself and the landscapes through which he travels. These landscapes themselves appear to become imbued with the political energy generated by Kim Il Sung, also becoming participants in the power which encourages the people around him. Kwon and Chung, thinking through the analysis of Max Weber, describe this power as charisma, which drives later North Korean politics by drawing authority and legitimacy from this very period. This power and energy produce a thick stream of affect meant to inspire and influence the reader. Exactly the same power serves to drive Kim Jong Suk closer to Kim Il Sung and transforms the landscapes where revolutionary politics are most frequently exercised. There is a sense of inevitability surrounding the eventual crossing of Kim Jong Suk and Kim Il-song's paths and the entwining of their political energies; the processes leading up to their encounter continue the transformation of Kim Jong Suk. In the next chapter Kim Jong Suk has broken the bounds of her past and is in the midst of transforming her own future and the future of others.

## CHAPTER FIVE

# Kim Jong Suk and the Transformation on Mount Paektu

She felt it would be impossible to be free from poverty and disgrace in such a world, and firmly resolved to fight against injustice to the end. (Anon. 2005, 14)

Kim Jong Suk died on 22 September 1949, aged thirty-two years old. In North Korean historiographic sources she is remembered by her husband as "an ardent revolutionary who devoted her all for the liberation of the country" and "whatever she did was for her comrades, not for herself". She died within four years of the Liberation of Korea, merely a year since North Korean state was founded and a full year before the outbreak of the Korean War (Anon. 2005, 268). She is a figure truly from the infancy of North Korean political form, coming to us as the faintest echo of the nation's initial foundation. Yet if a traveller to Pyongyang gets a chance to visit the Revolutionary Martyrs Cemetery, one of the holiest political grounds in that land, they will see no commemorative monuments dedicated to people who died in the Korean War of 1950–53. Instead, the sacred architecture memorialises those who fell during the pre-Liberation period. It is vital for North Korea to connect these historically disconnected activists to its newly imagined community (Anderson 1983), generated after 1945. The memorialising of this group of people itself is an important new invented tradition (Hobsbawm and Ranger 1983) for this community. The visitor of course today will certainly notice that the largest and most prominent of all the memorials and graves, at the fulcrum of the site's architecture, is that of Kim Jong Suk. North Korean politics and cultural memory hold this woman as not simply a vital revolutionary figure, but almost an immortal. The previous chapter recounted Kim Jong Suk's childhood and youth. In this chapter we discuss her transformation into a mature revolutionary by North Korean writers in political and historical narrative. Finally, through all these narratives, Kim Jong Suk has reached adulthood.

In Chapter Four the reader encountered a young Kim Jong Suk confronted with familial and social troubles common to many Korean rural households of the late nineteenth and the early twentieth century. Kim Jong Suk and others like her had struggled with the economic and social structures of the late Yi dynasty, but these structures were turned upside down through the encounter with modernity. The national landscape of the Korean peninsula was subjected to enormous and overwhelming challenges presented by new forms of economic development, extraction and accumulation. These changes challenged the ancient status quo of Korean government and politics, despite its attempts at reform and reconfiguration. Japanese colonialism also let loose new urgent forces upon Korean social and productive terrains, with families and communities such as that of Kim Jong Suk forced out and off their land by an influx of new landowners (Caprio 2014). Japanese owners sought to reconfigure Korean agricultural landscapes under new economic prerogatives, and such reconfigurations did not always include traditional Korean agricultural practices (Fedman 2015). Resistance to the new modes of being was treated very harshly and families, such as that of Kim Jong Suk as presented in the narratives of her biographies and hagiographies, were forced to flee and retreat to the margins of the Korean peninsula and beyond.

This diasporic community of Koreans would be key to the politics which has produced modern Korea. People inspired by the possibilities of capitalism and hostile to communism, including social democrats, sought refuge in the USA, China and elsewhere (Cumings 2005). They would also find ways of accommodating themselves to Japanese modernity, and later be deeply involved in the construction of the industrial and economic base of South Korea (Em 2013). Another camp sought to overthrow the Japanese power, historical forms of social hierarchy and the new processes of capitalism. They hunkered down in cities across Asia, especially in the Russian Far East and Manchuria (later Japanese occupied Manchukuo). Kim Il Sung was in this second group. Those who surrounded him harnessed the support of political actors that sought the diminution of Japanese power in the region, particularly the Soviet Union, optimistic about the possibilities for spreading revolution on its eastern fringes.

In the narratives related in this chapter follow Kim Jong Suk into the spaces of political resistance where she continues her dramatic transformation from child of colonial oppression to full-blown participant in revolutionary mythography. This narrative is rich in the political colour that marks North Korea's historiography. An important assertion of this book is that, within the narrative of Kim Jong Suk, personal agency and power are transferred between the human and the topographical. This interaction so characteristic of East Asian landscapes connects to the culture of immortality described in Chapter Three. Immortality culture conceives of a human as a model of a cosmos. The cosmos is often represented in a shape of a mountain. Mountain mirrors a human body;

rivers and waterfalls on a mountain parallel blood vessels and *ki* (氣) channels in a human body. The body of a human and the body of a mountain talk to each other: there is interaction and mutual co-influence. In contemporary North Korean narrative the transfer of personal agency and power between the human and the topographical supports the transformation of Kim Jong Suk into an immortal or a mountain goddess of sorts. Within the narrative the mountain reacts to revolutionary struggle, and nature itself supports, mirrors and reflects this struggle. Mt Paektu helps Kim Jong Suk and her fellow revolutionaries to contest Japanese power by providing shelter, food and medicine herbs; the lively active matter of Mt Paektu projects energy into current North Korean politics.[35]

## The Emergence of Kim Jong Suk

According to North Korean narratives and invented traditions, Kim Jong Suk's emergence into the revolutionary movement was meteoric. Members of the political movement she joined after the educational and personal epiphanies described in Chapter Four apparently "marvelled at her wits, audacity and resourcefulness". By the middle of September 1931 Kim Jong Suk, still only fourteen years old, had become a member of the Children's Vanguard, described as a "paramilitary organization of young people and children formed by Kim Il Sung". Later in that month, in what the narrative holds as something of a public coming out for a new revolutionary star, Kim Jong Suk is described as having roused passions during a meeting focused on the Manchurian Incident and Japan's annexation of north-eastern China with her first key piece of oratory.

> Why should our parents perish with bitterness in their hearts in this rough foreign land without seeing their beloved homeland? Why should our young people wither away, shedding tears and blood in the midst of these hardships? What is the cause of all these miseries, and who are to blame for these misfortunes? It is the Japanese marauders occupying our country and the fiendish landowners who are to blame. They are our sworn enemies. Without destroying them, none of us will be able to live in peace. Let all of us turn out as one, in the fight against the Japanese imperialists. (Anon. 2005, 17)

---

[35]  As mentioned in the Introduction, in the twenty-first century the political scientist Jane Bennett developed a theory of lively, active matter, talking about the active participation of non-human forces in events (Bennett 2010).

The Kim Jong Suk's audience are recounted to have been "Roused by her speech, the people shouted, raising clenched fists: Down with the Japanese imperialists and the wicked landowners!" Similar agitation was undertaken by Kim Jong Suk among female peasants as she critiqued methods and modes of their work for landlords. In particular, exploitation by the landowner of her (then) home village of Fuyandong was laid bare by her analysis, resulting in a "forest of sticks, hoes, rakes and sickles raised by the peasants [that] threatened the landowner who was brought to his knees" (Anon. 2005, 18).

This book has already asserted the importance of the transformative process and the technologies of self utilised to support it in Kim Jong Suk's narrative (Foucault et al. 1988). This transformation is an embodied technological process wrought upon herself and the selves of those closest to her. Her exposure to the perceived injustices of Japanese imperialism and landowner exploitation of the peasantry is itself transformational, in particular the disruptive moments that have marked out her family's interaction with authorities. These injustices are used as technological devices by the author(s) of the narrative to drive Kim Jong Suk's transformation. Equally, the process of cultural and political education through which she would be inculcated and absorbed into the revolutionary movement were the means of transformation. However, the primary vector in Kim Jong Suk's transformation from young peasant girl to Korean revolutionary nationalist was her experience of moments of extreme violence. These moments of violence are themselves technologies of self, applied upon the corporate body politic of North Korea. It is through this body that Kim Jong Suk is transformed by these technologies into a new self, into the immortal that the reader has seen her becoming. Beyond acts of physical violence, the violence of family separation and dislocation has played a key role in narrative memory and memorialisation, but now it will deployed on her own body.

The previous chapter touched upon past moments of brutality and inequity meted out on the peninsula's peasantry by its traditional oppressors, the landowning class, and by new landowners during the colonial period. Of course these brutalities are direct technologies of oppression deployed by those seeking to control groups of citizens such as Kim Jong Suk. These moments do indeed touch upon her immediate family, but at this point in her life violence comes much closer to her person. One moment in particular, occurring around July 1932, was the attack on Fuyandong by Japanese forces, directed at suppressing agitation and revolutionary anti-colonial and anti-landlord groups.

The Japanese soldiers attacking Fuyandong apparently set fire to the village, including Kim Jong Suk's own house. Upon arriving at her burning house she found her sister-in-law dead and her mother dreadfully burnt. In spite of her mother's last words having been "take revenge on the enemy for me", Kim Jong Suk was momentarily confused, momentarily distraught, "the thought of bringing up my infant nephew in this harsh world dazed me as if the sky had fallen in, as if the earth had sunk into an abyss" (Anon. 2005, 19). This technological or literary device of the narrative ruptures the bounds of social possibility for Kim and forces her to adopt revolutionary political means, making alternate modes of being impossible. However, it is also the loss and brutality of the moment that dramatically transform Kim Jong Suk, and shape and drive her political commitment. She turns away from such forms of resistance as education, agitation and distribution of leaflets to more direct revolutionary modes of action, such as guerrilla warfare. "The consciousness of the revolution helped me to rise", she recounted, and the text asserts that "unyielding struggle and punishing the enemy without mercy was the only way to wreak vengeance for the deaths of her parents and other family members" (Anon. 2005, 19)

Kim Jong Suk was forced to leave the bounds of familial connections and 'normal' life behind when she joined the Young Communist League on 25 July 1932 to begin the combat phase of her resistance. Her final transformation from member of her blood family to member of a political family is marked by giving up responsibility for the baby nephew she has been caring for since her sister-in-law was killed. Her own brother demands that she give up the child, asserting as he took it out of her arms that:

> You're not yet fully determined to fight for the revolution. If you are going to be a revolutionary, you must first think of the revolution. If you worry about your family, how can you make a revolution? Don't worry about the family [...] go and fight. (Anon. 2005, 20)

In the period when Kim Jong Suk was heavily involved in the Children's Corps of the Young Communist League the narrative takes effort to mould her image in a way similar to how it was later formed on the slopes of Mt Paektu. While she has left her familial commitments behind, it appears important for the writers of the text to continue asserting her conventional female character tropes. Kim Jong Suk, even at the height of this period of struggle, loved caring for children: "for her love for the children [...] in the guerrilla zone and her self-sacrificing devotion to them, she was loved and respected by them" (Anon. 2005, 24). However, it is clear that the children under Kim Jong Suk's care are not to be exempted nor excused from revolutionary activity, for education that Kim gave to the children included political inculcation. This political activity echoes her own technologies of self and technologies of resistance, instilling a commitment similar to her own:

> Kim Jong Suk also hardened the children through the revolutionary struggle. Revolutionary practice is a school for training people as revolutionaries, she said, and emphasized that only when the children were hardened through work and struggle from their early years could they become true

revolutionaries, capable of breaking through all difficulties and trials. (Anon. 2005, 22)

These children were to repeat Kim's own experience. They would not be simply targets of pedagogical practice, but combatants exposed to danger, to be transformed by similar moments of violence: "the children sometimes carried ammunition to the trenches on embattled hills and rolled down rocks upon the 'punitive' troops who were climbing up the hills" (Anon. 2005, 22).

Besides Kim Jong Suk's feminine or maternal qualities (even if couched in revolutionary terms), the narratives assert her seemingly superhuman abilities to resist pain or discomfort. Kim Jong Suk was able to work harder than others and to cope with hunger: "Hurrying about here and there every day, she often had to skip a meal. She bore all this, however, without any sign of fatigue" (Anon. 2005, 21). In another instance the owner of a house where she was staying has found her after a long day of work "washing the clothes of guerrillas at the riverside, even forgetting to have her supper". The host's response is intriguing: "holding and feeling her wet hands in his, the host was surprised at how coarse they were. Although her hands were severely chapped and calloused, she endured the pain with a sense of pride" (Anon. 2005, 21).

Kim Jong Suk's abilities to resist pain and endure physical suffering, combined with her prowess at guerrilla and war fighting in spite of her young age, are also highlighted in the texts. An example of this tendency is a text describing the events of the early 1930s when Kim Jong Suk and some of her fellow Children's Corps members are pinned down by Japanese 'punitive' forces in a snowstorm. During this altercation one of her fellow members, a boy who has claimed that he "would wreak vengeance upon the enemy for the deaths of his parents", disappears and is found being chased and about to be caught by a Japanese soldier. Kim Jong Suk, the narrative recounts, "dodged behind a rock and waited until the soldier had passed. Then she leapt from her hiding place and felled the enemy with two blows of a wooden club" (Anon. 2005, 24).

## Kim Jong Suk and the Road to and Beyond Mount Paektu

The narrative is now at the point where Kim Jong Suk grows beyond the bounds of the Children's Corps. North Korean sources describe Kim Jong Suk as having moved to the Chechangzi area after a period of real strife when diasporic Koreans and the various resistance movements in Manchuria were subjected to famine and disruption at the hands of Imperial Japan's forces. In

September 1935, in Chechangzi, Kim Jong Suk was admitted to the Korean People's Resistance Army (KPRA), Kim Il Sung's band of adult guerrillas.

Kim Jong Suk's entry into the KPRA is marked by distinct connections with historical and nationalist symbolism: "in front of the red flag fluttering in the sky of Chechangzi, she was awarded a rifle bearing the wishes of fallen comrades and the expectations of the Korean nation". Kim Jong Suk herself remarks on these symbolic elements with a quotation repeated many times in North Korean literature:

> With this rifle bearing the blood of the revolutionary forerunners and the people's desire for national liberation, I will be faithful to General Kim Il Sung to the last moment of my life. I take this one rifle as one hundred rifles and will shoot one bullet as one hundred bullets to take revenge on the enemy. (Anon. 2005, 45)

Kim Jong Suk's transformation through war and combat continues during her time in the KPRA and culminates on the slopes of Mt Paektu. North Korean mythography deploys her skill and adeptness at taking "revenge on the enemy" as key features of the story in the period preceding the events around Mt Paektu. Intense violence again marks the narratives of this period, for instance while crossing the Godong River:

> the guerrillas discharged a volley of bullets when the main column of the enemy troops was in the middle of the bridge. The bridge was covered with the corpses of the enemy soldiers in an instant. Kim Jong Suk hit with a single shot a Japanese officer who was commanding his men with a sword. (Anon. 2005, 46)

Later in January 1936 Kim Jong Suk again attacks the Japanese with fatal accuracy: "Kim Jong Suk fought at the salient of the height that bore the brunt of the battle. Four hundred metres down from the height, an enemy officer was leading a charge. She killed the officer with a single shot" (Anon. 2005, 49).

Against the background of the blood-soaked, aggressive atmosphere of the KPRA's activities, the text highlights Kim Jong Suk's feminine or maternal characteristics. She is a devoted wife willing to put herself in danger for the sake of her husband Kim Il Sung, serving as his bodyguard. The narrative describes the events as follows:

> Kim Il Sung commanded the battle from a rock on the ridge of the mountain. Mindful of his safety, Kim Jong Suk kept a close watch on the surroundings. Noticing reeds swaying strangely, she turned her eyes and saw half a dozen enemy soldiers hiding in a reed field, taking aim at Kim Il Sung on the ridge [...] at the hair-raising moment, Kim Jong Suk raced to Kim Il Sung, shouting "Comrade Commander!" and shielding him with her body. Then

she pulled the trigger of her Mauser. The enemy soldier in the front fell down, dropping his gun. A gunshot followed. Kim Il Sung had shot over her shoulder. In this way they both shot all the enemy soldiers in the reed field dead (Anon. 2005, 165).

This linguistic formula is intriguingly repeated in the description of the battle in the forest at Huanggouling in October 1940.[36] "Kim Jong Suk shot the enemy machine-gunner to death, covering Kim Il Sung with her body as she did so. 'Comrade Commander! It is dangerous here. You must leave here.' It was really a hair-raising moment" (Anon. 2005, 132). Kim Jong Suk, already a figure of considerable acclaim, is transformed by these events, moving towards a charismatic, saintly status, marked by selflessness, concern for the person of Kim Il Sung and for the continuation of the revolution.

In Korean historical context, dying for the sake of a husband, in order to benefit his family or protect a family honour, was considered a rarely practised but important obligation of the Confucian wife. Such behaviour was rated exemplary in the early Chosŏn dynasty: a virtuous wife named Kim, just like Kim Jong Suk, shot with a bow and arrows a tiger attacking her husband, almost shielding him with her body. This popular illustrated story forms a part of the Samgang Haengsildo (三綱行實圖, Illustrated Exemplars of the Three Bonds),[37] commissioned in 1428 by King Sejong (1418–50) for the purpose of 'popular education' and printed using woodblocks in 1434 (Kim 2012, 225, 228, 232).

As we have mentioned before, Kim Jong Suk is presented as having a real commitment to the safety and care of children. In the narrative the KPRA was accompanied by the families of the fighters, including their children and the children of those who had lost their lives in battle. However, the children were not well cared for given the difficulties of war, so Kim Jong Suk made it her business to improve their lot. She "had charge of dozens of children […] had to take care of sick children and patch their threadbare clothes". Kim Jong Suk's maternal characteristics filled with a sense of selflessness and sacrifice suggest a superhuman, semi-immortal nature. This is particularly acute when applied to her abstinence from normal eating and sustenance patterns: "Kim Jong Suk herself dug out grass roots from the snow-covered ground and picked berries

---

[36]  Reiteration of linguistic formulas, as seen here in North Korean texts, is a technique utilised in various spiritual and religious traditions around the world. Repetitions serve to continuously programme the reader at both the conscious and unconscious levels, and aid memorisation, similar to mantras and prayers.

[37]  The Three Bonds describe the three social structures, the three ethical obligations of loyalty and servitude. The subject must serve the king, the son or daughter must serve the parent, and the wife must serve the husband. Thus formulated, moral and social obligations show that women were traditionally included among the subjects of virtue in East Asia.

to feed the children. Many times she had only water for her own meal" (Anon. 2005, 51). In East Asian tradition, self-transformation through pain, suffering and self-sacrifice is often a necessary step on the way to immortality, and Kim Jong Suk follows this pattern in her narrative. Here a practice of immortality can be identified: an adherent refrains from eating, later drinks only water and at last feeds solely on the air (Vasilyev 1970).

Another technological element of Kim Jong Suk's transformation within the narrative connects back to the river crossings recounted in Chapter Four. There, she crosses rivers as a young child, moving into a place where she can be transformed from a subject of colonial pressure into a politically active young person. The present chapter discusses Kim's crossing into the transformative territory of Mt Paektu, sacred to North Korean historiography and mythology: "This wonderful natural fortress stretching from the summit of Mt Paektu, the ancestral mountain of our country, will provide us with a theatre of our sacred future struggle" (Anon. 2005, 61).

Kim Jong Suk's exploits on the mountain have generated memorial architecture on this territory (Chi 2004). The areas on Mt Paektu and in its vicinity are held to be camps and overnight resting areas established by Kim Jong Suk and her female guerrilla band (Rodong Sinmun 2016). Memorial architecture includes cooking and firepit places where Kim Jong Suk is attested to have cooked dinner for her fellow fighters (Rodong Sinmun 2016). Tree trunks and stones have slogans and political graffiti inscribed on them, again considered to have been left by Kim Jong Suk and others (Rodong Sinmun 2016). North Korea's current political texts hold these sites to be historically accurate and authentic. These cooking sites and camps are believed to be the actual physical spaces where Kim Jong Suk and her fellows interacted. The 'slogan trees' are covered by a transparent plastic wrapping, whereas the cooking areas are protected with wooden and glass structures. These sacred objects are designed to emphasise the efforts taken towards preserving them and to articulate the stories behind them.

North Korean media regularly refers to ritual visits by groups of school children and bureaucrats to these sites, and such visits perform educative, pedagogic and training functions. The construction of the architecture and infrastructure designed to make such tours comfortable (hotels, railway lines, stations and places to eat) is also regularly highlighted in the media (Rodong Sinmun 2015a–c, 2016). The power and charisma of Kim Jong Suk and her fellow guerrillas is reactivated at these moments and incorporated into contemporary lives of the visitors (Winstanley-Chesters 2015). By the process of scaling and rescaling the events memorialised by the sites, contemporary North Koreans are transformed anew by bringing the energy of the past into their own lives and practices.

According to North Korean mythological narrative, Kim Jong Il, the father of the current leader Kim Jong Un, was born to Kim Il Sung and Kim Jong Suk in a secret camp at the base of Mt Paektu. North Korea has directed much political effort at messaging and propaganda regarding the infrastructure that surrounds political tourism to the 'Paektu Secret Camp'. The initial versions of the narrative recount battles between guerrillas and the Japanese. In reality, these battles were not in the vicinity of Mt Paektu: the *Works* of Kim Il Sung as published in the late 1960s and early 1970s place the most important emphasis on the military altercation between Kim Il Sung's guerrilla band and Japanese forces at a police outpost in Poch'ŏn County, an area to the south of Mt Paektu. Other battles in Changbai and Antu counties across the border in Manchukuo are also important to the narrative of this period.[38] Later in North Korean historiography these events were shifted closer to Mt Paektu, and then placed directly upon the mountain in acts of historical reconstruction. Later works from the 1980s and 1990s, such as Kim Il-song's autobiography *Reminiscences (With the Century)* (1992) and the *Biography of Kim Jong Suk* (first published in 1991) reconfigure the historical narrative, placing new incidences on and around Mt Paektu. These works blur the narrative's geographical clarity so in the end it is no longer understandable in which counties these important events took place, and not even clear if they happened in the territory of Korea at all: these traditions and narratives become invented anew once again. As a new location of the battles, Mt Paektu thus becomes vitally important to the narrative. Such historical shifts are of course not recorded in the current version of North Korean historiography, nor in the life stories of those involved. The constructed, recreated and partly imagined narratives picture this small collection of log cabins situated at the foot of Mt Paektu as vitally important for their resistance and survival, and so the mountain and the landscape of the cabins are reimagined and reborn as a new sort of mountain: as Debarbieux and Rudaz (2015) would understand, a political mountain. This mountain's material presence is made active and lively by its intersection with politics and historical ideology (Bennett 2010), and here the sense of North Korean politics and nationhood is born. The historiography recounts that the camp underneath Mt Paektu made a future Korean revolution possible and secured the success of the group led by the Kims. This camp, now singularly immortalised in the constructed historiography, was initially but one of a collection of secret guerrilla camps all around the mountain. The text of Kim Jong Suk's biography admits that:

---

[38] Known historically as Manchuria, the territory was invaded and occupied by the Japanese Empire in 1931 and functioned as the puppet Kingdom of Manchukuo under Emperor Puyi, the last of the Qing dynasty, between 1932 and 1945. It was invaded and occupied by the Soviet Union in August 1945, before control was handed over to Chinese Communist forces in 1946. It is now part of the People's Republic of China.

other secret camps were built in many places in the Mt Paektu area, such as Saja Peak, Mt Kom, Mt Sono, Mt Kanbaek, Mudu Hill and Soyonji Peak. In the west Jiandao area, satellite secret camps were built in Heixiazigou, Diyangzi, Erdaogang, Hengshan, Limingshui, Fuhoushui, Qingfeng, and other places. (Anon. 2005, 63)

According to the texts, Kim Jong Suk was at the centre of all these camps' activities. Having arrived at each camp she helped the rapid construction of the camp facilities and continued her own military training to become, as the narratives often describe her, a "crackshot". Kim Jong Suk transforms herself into a warrior, ready to mete out violent ends to her enemies. For example, in an initially light-hearted after-dinner conversation at the Paektu camp Kim states that:

If I fail to kill the enemy at the first shot, the enemy will kill me. Moreover, we accompany the General in dangerous situations. So I am always enthusiastic about shooting practice, striving to kill the enemy with one bullet, no matter when or where he may appear. (Anon. 2005, 63)

The insistence of Kim Jong Suk and her fellow guerrillas that they should be Kim Il Sung's "bullet proof vest", and think nothing of the annihilation of their own bodies for the needs of the revolution, would soon be put to the test on Mt Paektu.

The female guerrillas who surrounded Kim Jong Suk also were outstanding warriors. Kim Hwak Sil, referred to as a "woman commander" by her colleagues and comrades was, similarly to Kim Jong Suk, a "crackshot" who "could hold a rifle by the barrel in each hand and lift them overhead" (Women of Korea 1990a, 25); Kim Il Sung himself presented her with a golden ring for "mowing down the enemy with a sharp-edged bayonet like an angry tigress, shouting out 'Enemies, Come on! I'm avenging my comrades with this bayonet'" (Women of Korea 1990a, 25). Pak Rok Gun was "as brave as a lion in battles [...] She walked more than 15km a day with a machine gun on her shoulders" (Women of Korea 1990b, 25) and Pak Su Hwan "fought bravely in many battles including those at Chechangzi and Naitoushan" (Women of Korea 1987a, 30).

Sometimes the deaths of Kim Jong Suk's fellow travellers are portrayed as acts of military significance: such is the case of Kim Hwak Sil. In March 1938, she encountered an attacking Japanese force having walked through "a field of shoulder-high purple eulalia". Hiding behind a rock, she was wounded in the chest and then ran out of ammunition. The North Korean journal *Women of Korea* describes her next move in some detail:

She disassembled the lock of her rifle and buried it under the snow so that the enemy could not deprive her of the rifle permeated with the blood and soul of her comrades in arms. Then she dashed into the enemy with hand grenades in her arms. An explosion shook the forest and the enemy was wiped out. (Women of Korea 1990a, 25)[39]

The violence enacted by Kim Hwak Sil on her own body and the bodies of her enemies (who no doubt died agonising deaths) becomes a key narrative and political device in the texts. It is meant to be transformative also for the readers of the text, with the disfigurement and destruction of these women's bodies at the hands of their Japanese enemies perhaps serving to illustrate for North Korean readers the potential violence to be enacted on themselves in the event of a future enemy victory. This episode with Kim Hwak Sil is by no means an isolated occurrence, for the reader also learns of brutality to fighters such as Pak Rok Gum, whose "torture was extremely cruel" (Women of Korea 1987c, 26); thrown in a room where patients "with epidemic diseases were kept" she "died of illness on October 16th, 1940 at the age of 25" (Women of Korea 1990b, 25).

The female warriors' torture and deaths are presented as powerful moments of witness. The dying women themselves testify to future revolutionary generations: while dying in prison Pak Rok Gum coined a song with the verse "the red flag of the masses/covers the corpse of the fighter/the blood dyes the flag/ before the corpse cools" (Women of Korea 1990b, 25). Suggesting the transfer and rescaling of charismatic nationalist power through the violent death of these fighters, their deaths are becoming moments of narrative transfiguration.

The female heroes' lives and deaths intertwine with Kim Jong Suk's own story. Choe Hui Suk, one of Kim Jong Suk's followers, was captured by a Japanese "punitive force" while taking a message to Kim Il Sung. She was badly wounded in the initial raid, and the texts describe in detail how she was subsequently tortured (Women of Korea 1986, 25); she died on 12 March 1941. The transformation of Kim Jong Suk and characters such as Choe projects a potentially vital message for North Korea's future citizens, who would read that subjugation of the life of the individual is a necessary step for the eventual success of the collective: Choe Hui Suk would not be able to witness the later commemoration of Kim Jong Suk following the various battles on Paektu, and in particular Kim's similar experience at the hands of a Japanese "punitive force". Kim Jong Suk was herself captured in August 1937 while travelling from the Paektu area to meet a women's group who had been

---

[39]  *Women of Korea* is the English-language edition of a famous North Korean journal devoted to women's matters. The New Korean edition is titled 조선 녀성 Choson Yosong (Chosŏn Yŏsŏng) and has been printed since the early 1960s. Although the English edition closed in the early 1990s, the Korean version continues in production to the present day. The Korean and English versions of the journal do not always include the same articles, but contain material which feeds off and influences each other.

offering support to the guerrilla fighters. She was incarcerated in Yaofangzi (now in Jilin Province, China) by operatives of Japanese counter-insurgency forces. "The enemy put her to bestial torture to take confession out of her" and her captors taunted her with assertions "that she would have to be ready for death" (Anon. 2005, 84). Kim Jong Suk is marched through a local village, the text recounting that her feet were bloody from physical punishment and "her whole body bearing traces of horrible torture and her white jacket and black skirt torn here and there" (Anon. 2005, 85).

Kim Jong Suk's survival from torture and pain is vital to the process of her transformation into a North Korean political and cultural immortal. In many cultures around the globe, including Christianity, passing through an ordeal is an important element in the attaining of sainthood. The text records that while Kim is being hauled through the village trailing her damaged body upon the ground, the residents remarked upon "her eyes full of strong will and wisdom all the time, shining with confidence and conviction". Kim Il Sung is even recorded as having exclaimed upon her release: "She was afire with love for the people. She thought her sacrifice for others was not in the least wasteful. It was her nature to go through even fire and water if it was for the sake of her comrades" (Anon. 2005, 86). Kim Jong Suk metamorphoses in the fires of torture and pain to become more than a human heroine, almost an immortal. Mt Paektu grants her some of its power, and in accepting this power Kim Jong Suk resembles traditional figures of *sanshin* and their worshippers: *sanshin*, spirits of the mountains, are themselves manifestations of the strength of the mountain, and those who pray on the mountain absorb this power into their minds and bodies. Thus, Kim Jong Suk embodies and demonstrates the power of the mountain, gaining an ability to transform herself and others. This transformation manifests both in her own survival from severe ordeals, and in her ability to heal her comrades by picking medicinal herbs growing on the mountain. Applying thse herbs to ailing warriors is a symbolical manifestation of harnessing the power of the mountain and incorporating it into the bodies of people.

A good example is the story of Jang Chol Gu. Jang, a guerrilla close to Kim Il Sung, is weighed so low by the travails of revolutionary combat that he becomes paralysed and semi-conscious. As the guerrilla band are traversing some thick forests near Mt Paektu, they must leave the incapacitated fighter behind. Kim Il Sung suggests Kim Jong Suk stays with the dying man to comfort him in his final moments, with the troop returning to pick her up later. Kim Jong Suk agrees to stay, but instead of simply witnessing Jang's expiration she takes it upon herself to heal him. At this point the narrative begins to refer to her as a healer and "surgeon". Using materials from the forest, in a series of acts suggestive of Korean traditional herbal culture, she starts to "gather pine and fir resins, which she pasted over Jang's swollen arm and the backs of his hands". Kim Jong Suk continued to "pluck wild fruits and medicinal herbs that could help reduce fever, boiled them overnight, and put spoonfuls of the boiled medicine into the mouth of the sick man" (Anon. 2005, 118). One day, deep in the forests underneath Mt Paektu, Kim Jong Suk even used her own body to fend off the cold of night and prevent further degradation in her patient's condition:

> Kim Jong Suk took off her jacket, and covered Jang with it and her own blanket. Yet, even the jacket and the blanket could not prevent the rain from soaking the patient. So Kim Jong Suk covered the patient with her body. (Anon. 2005, 118)

> Eyes glaring at the raging rainstorm in the night sky and her mouth moving in time to a song, she reminded me of an invincible fighter, as fierce as a tiger, engaged in a do-or-die battle with the enemy. Her noble image greatly moved me. (Anon. 2005, 119)

The recollections of the recovered Jang Chol Gu, nursed back to health in the forests of Mt Paektu, give an extraordinary account of Kim's appearance at this moment. In her apparent invincibility, Kim Jong Suk has become a semi-immortal; her power and energy have developed beyond human. Kim's devotion to the cause of Korean revolutionary nationalism, her passionate resistance to Japanese imperialism, would further her transformation in the years leading up to the collapse of Japanese power in the Pacific region in 1945. The Liberation of the Korean peninsula in 1945 and Kim Jong Il's birth mark just one stage in the progression of North Korea's historical narrative, within which the roots of Kim Jong Suk's future image can be found. At the moment of North Korea's foundation, a developing sense of mythology surrounding Kim Jong Suk in the landscape of Mt Paektu, and her future embedding into Pyongyang's pantheon of revolutionary heroes, was already under way.


## Kim Jong Suk Beyond Paektu

Kim Jong Suk was transformed into a warrior at Mt Paektu. The cultural and political landscapes of the Korean nationalist revolution made her a teacher of other guerrillas, and she also becomes a healer: "Legends have it that 'the woman general of Mt Paektu employs the art of shrinking space and has mastered the art of changing her shape. She makes the enemy blind by using magical power" (Anon. 2005, 158). The ability to modify space, change shape, blind enemies, etc., are classical attributes of East Asian immortals, so these legends surrounding Kim Jong Suk's combat on the periphery of colonial Chosen are vital for her later political canonisation. Her transformation in the narrative began at the moment when nation building in Korea followed the collapse of Japanese power in 1945. Although the Liberation was in August 1945, it would not be until November that year that Kim Jong Suk and some of her guerrilla attendants left the training base where they had seen out the last period of colonial rule. Kim Jong Suk journeyed from colonial Chosen to the diasporic world of struggle as a young guerrilla; she crossed back into the territory of newly independent Korea (though not yet North Korea at this point), as a seasoned warrior:

> Kim Jong Suk standing on the deck side by side with her son Kim Jong Il felt that the mountain range of the homeland, in the morning sunshine, was approaching to welcome them. "Comrades," she shouted, "I can see the homeland over there, the homeland!"

In this newly independent sovereign space, Kim Jong Suk's efforts would be translated from practice into mythic narrative, and the moment of trans-formation and 'recrossing' is visceral.[40] "Scalding tears were trickling down Kim Jong Suk's cheeks. How much she had yearned to see the land of her forefathers! Not for a moment had she forgotten her homeland during so many years of desperate battles" (Anon. 2005, 160).

Kim Jong Suk and her compatriots arrived at the damaged port of Sonbong to be greeted by an initially small contingent of veterans of the anti-Japanese struggle. According to the narrative, Kim Jong Suk could not even make it off the wharf and breakwater before the first ripples of her legend and mythical status began to catch up with her:

> there spread among the people, a rumour that the woman talking with the anti-Japanese veterans was the famous woman general from Mt Paektu, Kim Jong Suk [...] The people were greatly excited to see with their own eyes the legendary anti-Japanese war heroine. An old woman came running from the crowd and embraced Kim Jong Suk. (Anon. 2005, 160)

Apparently, it was not just the common people who revered the legendary character. Kim Jong Suk was also beset with interview requests from local media who were keen to "hear how, she, a woman, had been able to fight and defeat the one million strong Japanese army in Manchuria". The *Biography* maintains that a number of pamphlets with titles such as *Plunged into the Revolutionary Movement as a Fourteen Year Old Girl of Fervour* and *The Woman Fighter Dedicates Half Her Life to Independence: Let Us Follow the Example of Her*

---

[40]  For the concept of recrossing see Chapter Six.

*Self-Sacrificing Spirit* were printed following the Liberation, the first elements of a legend which glorified and memorialised Kim Jong Suk.

Kim Jong Suk herself would not live much beyond the very early period of an independent Korea and would experience only a year of the existence of North Korea. Presumably the physical impact of many years of fighting, struggle, frugality and deprivation took their toll on her body. The element of her character mythologised as an almost supernatural ability to endure pain in order to better support or protect other people around her is evident in the narrative of her final day: "On September 21, 1949 Kim Il Sung set out on the road of on-the-spot-guidance to meet the people of Thosan County [...] Kim Jong Suk sent him off at the front gate as usual.[41] Her manner and parting words were as in ordinary times, but her health was in a critical condition." Kim Jong Suk made precisely no mention of this and not only "said farewell to him with a bright smile" but "endured the pain she felt to finish a woollen jacket she had been knitting for Kim Il Sung" (Anon. 2005, 267).


## Kim Jong Suk as Charismatic Immortal

The celebration in 2014 of the ninety-seventh anniversary of Kim Jong Suk's birth showed that as a seemingly immortal revolutionary she still is a key part of North Korea's regime authority and legitimacy. In Chapter One I outlined the various analytic approaches to contemporary North Korean politics and ideology: this section briefly touches on the theoretical background through which I encounter such ideology within the country's political and material landscapes.

The North Korean political landscape is not traditionally East Asian in the sense described in Chapter Three. However, a focus on the achievement of immortality through self-development and transformation is found not only in written political narratives, for the paintings and imagery of North Korea also follow traditional examples of East Asian artistic expressions of immortality. Such artistic claims and projections of immortality play a key role within the political culture and narrative of the nation, with images of Kim Il Sung and Kim Jong Il to be found everywhere in North Korea: in most town and city squares, on the walls of important buildings, in each subway carriage, in offices and in every citizen's house. These images are cyphers for the power of politics in North Korea, the authority of its history and the immortality of

---

[41]  'On-the-spot-guidance' refers to the method of governance in North Korea. The Leader (Kim Il Sung, Kim Jong Il or Kim Jong Un) visits a facility or farm and announces new strategies or principles for particular development. This method was also popular in the Soviet Union, Cuba and China.

its founders and revolutionary heroes. Similar to religious artistic artefacts, these paintings are in some way inhabited by the personhood represented upon them; to damage these objects, desecrate them or even to fail to prevent damage or insult is to directly denigrate the leaders themselves (KCNA 2013).

Koen de Ceuster notes the inherently political nature of North Korean art, contesting analysis which holds art undertaken or produced under totalitarian forms of politics to be impossible. He frames such production within a more reflexive system in which art and artists function as part of a collaborative, "social body" (Golomstock 1990; de Ceuster 2011), marked and influenced by the nature of politics and ideology. Art within this corporate body serves purposes beyond individual production and creativity, helping to uplift and educate, to form a person towards a certain 'ideal'. Medieval East Asian paintings in a similar way embodied the immortality pursuits of the painters and the viewers, educating and uplifting. Paintings produced within this context therefore form part of political, cultural and historical narratives and constitute technologies of the self, in Michel Foucault's language.

The author of this book follows de Ceuster's recent analysis of a number of North Korean paintings (2015), which notes important axes and configurations within the images. Figures within seemingly mundane paintings of families and home life are connected through invisible lines of power and energy to ideologically important elements found within the pictures. This is certainly true when it comes to paintings of this book's particular mountain immortal, Kim Jong Suk, and her husband-to-be. There is a famous painting of her crossing the mountains to contest Japanese power during winter; fellow guerrillas struggle through waist-deep snow yet the future Great Leader appears to rise above the drifts. Similarly, Kim Jong Suk features in a series of paintings unperturbed by the deep level of leaf litter, nimble in spite of difficult ground and able to resist and survive Japanese attack from multiple directions. Both Kim Il Sung and Kim Jong Suk are pictured as not being impacted by snow and leaves, rising ethereally above the difficult landscape while being deeply committed to the efforts of their comrades around them. The images suggest the radical difference in power of both Kims from normal participants: as mountain immortals they are somehow on a different plane of reality.

The battles represented by the paintings are important for North Korean history; these paintings stand as active elements of written constructed narratives. Kim Jong Suk is also featured in a number of portraits: a deeper view would reveal a landscape of cultural and political importance, vital to Kim Jong Suk's own history. There in the background is Mt Paektu; Kim Jong Suk stands next to Lake Samjiyon, an important battle site during the colonial period; on her left are the birch trees under which her relationship with her future husband, Kim Il Sung, was acknowledged for the first time by North Korean historical narratives. Mt Paektu, the lake and the birch trees thus become important elements participating in her depiction and immortalisation. They remind us of traditional paintings with elements of auspicious clouds, lone pine trees, vertical stone slabs, animals, and birds (Munakata 1991, 36–41) which are usually drawn on the picture of a sacred mountain, a symbol and embodiment of immortality.

Along with the narratives presented within North Korean texts, the paintings of Kim Jong Suk serve multiple roles. First, they are commemorative material fitting within the wider structures of North Korean politics, which might be termed the personality cult underpinning the Kim dynasty. Secondly they serve as educational material for North Korean historical narratives of the revolutionary period. However, in the light of de Ceuster's work this book suggests that the narratives, their emplacement and the organisation of the images serve to emphasise elements of power and energy directed at the transformation of the self, just like traditional East Asian paintings of immortals and sacred mountains. The 'self' transformed within the narrative is that of Kim Jong Suk, changing from a young Korean girl into a revolutionary leader, from mortal into immortal. But there the transformation does not end but starts. The landscape involved is also transforming; the potential viewers become incorporated within this transformation, participate themselves in this powerful cultural and political production. A similar process happens when a dynamic representation of a sacred mountain in traditional East Asian paintings influences and transforms the viewer. The value and the goal of North Korean narratives and images is to transform the minds and bodies of the viewers, to take them down the path of revolution and ideological inspiration. This is how the images of Kim Jong Suk on Mt Paektu adopt, continue and develop the ancient East Asian tradition of depicting mountain immortality, directed at the transformation of the viewer. They also reflect the traditions of alchemy discussed in Chapter Three. This is a political or ideological alchemy, through which the mind or the will of the viewer is forged into a more precious or useful material, important to the needs of North Korea's revolution.

Denis Cosgrove (1984), Noel Castree (2001) and Benjamin Joinau (2014) have already discussed the problem of constructed or created political landscapes in North Korea. This book of course also bears in mind the landmark work of Heonik Kwon and Byung-ho Chung (2012) on the theatricality of North Korean contemporary politics. It utilises Kwon and Chung's thesis, along with analysis inspired by Cosgrove and Castree, that North Korean political narrative directed at strengthening the charismatic role of the leader necessarily begets a mythological landscape with a Kim dynasty as a primary actor within that landscape. Kim Jong Suk and Kim Il Sung's role in the narratives serves as a primary example of the action of the political charisma and theatrics within a landscape. In this charismatic frame, Kim Jong Suk's transformation follows traditional notions of human being becoming divine, achieving immortality – notions we outlined before. The artefacts visually representing this culture are traditional East Asian paintings of mountains. The landscape in the pictures is represented as being in motion, it comes alive and transforms the viewer. Thus the processes of producing and viewing the painting become technologies of the self directed at the achievement of immortality. The motifs of visually representing *ki*, the traditional East Asian life energy, are key elements in painting sacred mountains, as we have described in Chapter Three. The vision of the universe as a dynamic function of *ki*, which is also life itself, is in line with the traditional East Asian understanding of the universe as living and sentient. In contemporary times, similar ideas have been articulated and theorised by the philosopher Jane Bennett, who coined the term 'vibrant matter' (Bennett 2010). In line with the idea that every thing is alive and every mountain and lake has a spirit of its own, Bennett suggests a "thing power" in which material objects and forces maintain and generate their own sense of agency, their own energy, which is also political in a sense that they act in their own interest. Kim Jong Suk co-opts some of the vibrancy of the surrounding landscape's materiality, pre-projecting and reconfiguring it for her own ends and means, just as an East Asian alchemist incorporates the energy of the sacred mountains into their own mind, heart and body.

The landscapes of contemporary North Korea, the Revolutionary Martyrs Cemetery and the various places associated with military and ideological power can be seen through a Cosgrovian lens as spaces in production, spaces of becoming, transformed and transforming through social practice. In Kim Jong Suk's case this was a practice of resistance and war fighting, of violence, survival, abstinence and combat. These transformations supported the invented traditions vital to the newly imagined community of North Korea, as much as the power of Kim Jong Suk's story. The transformation we have already seen in the young Kim Jong Suk through her interactions with the vibrant or lively physical, social and cultural spaces of Korean colonialism and diasporic exploitation essentially has been brought about by such praxis. Through these struggles Kim Jong Suk has been brought by the narrative to a charismatic, deified state, continuing and further developing Korean and East Asian cults of immortality.

## Framing Kim Jong Suk Against the Topography of Mount Paektu

This chapter essentially concludes this book's review of the legends of North Korea's 'new goddess on Mt Paektu'. For this book and its author this legendary woman, Kim Jong Suk, exists in North Korea's mythology as an ideologically skewed avatar reminiscent of ancient East Asian immortals. She exemplifies the pursuit of immortality, a technology of the self in the language of Michel Foucault, demonstrative of different stages on this path. Kim Jong Suk is a human being yet transitioning from mortality towards immortality. She aspires to encourage self-perfection in others and for this purpose various technologies of transformation, and Kim Jong Suk's story itself, serve as just such a technology. This process of pursuing immortality for the self and for the other is directly connected to the transformation of this equally legendary North Korean topography.

As reviewed in Chapter Three, the special genre of painting sacred mountains is a part of a culture of immortality in East Asia. Sacred mountains in East Asian paintings of immortals are alive and breathing. Despite the fact that the picture itself is static – a painting, not a video – the topography is presented as dynamic in these images. The curves of the mountain connote the feeling of transformation, people ascending the mountain are in motion, the picture often shows the wind blowing, an attribute of divine presence. In the pictures a mountain symbolises a human body as a microcosm, i.e. a mini-model of the universe. The fluid, flowing, active topography of a mountain shows the changes in a human body taking place as part of the usual functioning of a living organism. Simultaneously this transforming topography represents the life of the universe, its never-ending change. However, the dynamic representation has also an additional meaning of the ascendance of a mortal body towards being and having an immortal body. Here can be seen a slow-moving technology of self, a gradual change, altering the very nature and essence of a living being. Transplanting this idea into the universe as a living and sentient being, it connotes the motif that the universe itself aspires to self-perfect and to become a better place. East Asian sectarian, millenarian, secret societies thus often linked self-perfection with the aspiration towards a new and better world, a tendency vividly present in the North Korean legends of Kim Jong Suk, and in other legends from that country.

For North Korea the transformation of landscape is a continuous process. North Korean politics is constantly repackaging Kim Jong Suk's mythology to suit new purposes and different situations. The landscape where she figures as the first wife of the national leader, Kim Il Sung, and the mother of his successor, Kim Jong Il, is also constantly recreated by North Korea's contemporary politics and practices. Through these processes, such spaces as the cooking facilities in the temporary camps and the birch trees under which she is imagined to have met Kim Il Sung become sacred architectures. Many of these particular pieces of topography form part of the actual landscape of the Mt Paektu region. The following chapter explores a little further some elements of this repackaging of traditions close to Kim Jong Suk, and some more recent reimaginations and reconstructions of North Korean revolutionary traditions and their connected and rescaled landscapes.

## CHAPTER SIX

# Beyond Mount Paektu: Crossings and Reterritorialisings

This chapter moves slightly beyond Mt Paektu, and in many ways slightly beyond Kim Jong Suk, in order to explore another aspect of North Korean topography and its connection with political narratives. The reader will hopefully remember the writing of Erik Swyngedouw (1997) and his theoretical reconstruction from cartography of ideas of scale and scaling to allow the reprojection of political narrative across space and time. The utility of Swyngedouw's concept is of course extremely applicable to North Korea, and these notions are determined not only by the daily practices of North Korean citizens (going to school and work, obtaining food, engaging in leisure activity), but also by the political elites of Pyongyang in their attempt to control the population. In North Korea these processes of scale and scaling are very much rhetorical practices as much as they are about impacting politically on social relations and utilising the charismatic energy described earlier through the work of Kwon and Chung across time as well as space. These processes are also used across space and time to implant Kim Jong Suk's legacy and memory in contemporary North Korea and to further construct the invented traditions which surround her.

This chapter in a sense returns to the moment in Kim Jong Suk's life when as an oppressed child she crossed the Amnok river to the lands of Manchuria to the north, which were a little more liminal and not yet part of Japan's colonial project. As I have said earlier in this book, crossings and recrossings of rivers are vital for North Korean historiography and ideology, allowing the key characters in the story to transform into something else, and then to be transformed on their return. This chapter focuses on those crossings and the invented traditions and transformations produced by and around them, which in many cases connect to contemporary journeys and traditions made in North Korea around Mt Paektu. This time, however, this chapter works through the theoretical lens provided by Gilles Deleuze and Felix Guattari in *Anti-Oedipus: Capitalism and Schizophrenia* (1984), and suggests that

North Korean invented traditions and theatric energies are rescaled across time and space through the processes of what Deleuze and Guattari termed 'deterritorialisation' and 'reterritorialisation'. Deleuze and Guattari used these notions to articulate the processes involved in the fracturing, collapse or disintegration of situated social and cultural bonds between a physical terrain and the population or culture that inhabited it. Much of their analysis revolves around the impact of capitalism on such cultural bonds, and the pressures that alienated communities from their territories and traditional homes. While these processes transform and sometimes deeply impact on such cultures, they do not necessarily eradicate them and they can re-form more powerfully or differently elsewhere. Deleuze and Guattari actually distinguish between absolute deterritorialisation, in which the object of the process is completely destroyed or negated, and relative deterritorialisation in which it reappears elsewhere or in a different moment.

Good examples of this in terms of imagined communities include two Eastern European visions of nationalism. Livonia and its language of Livonian was originally a pagan territory of Balto-Finnic people roughly occupying what is now northern Latvia and southern Estonia. Once a powerful coastal trading nation which controlled the Daugava River, Livonia was devastated during the Livonian Crusade of 1198–1209 (the last campaign for mass conversion of a population in Europe), and never really recovered its position (Zajas 2013). Estonia was also the territory of another Balto-Finnic people long subsumed into more powerful nations such as Lithuania, Poland, Russia and Sweden. Estonia's moment of independence before 1945 was also brief, nineteen years from 1920 to 1939. Estonia and the notion of being an Estonian was deterritorialised for many centuries under earlier rulers, and from 1939 to 1991 by Nazi Germany and the Soviet Union (according to Estonian historiography), yet in 2020 there is a vibrant and energetic Estonian state, a member of the European Union, famous for its tech-savvy democracy. Its deterritorialisation was only relative (Peiker 2016); Livonia on the other hand would never rise again from underneath the memory or curtain of another state. Today only 250 residents of Latvia and thirty residents of Estonia claim to be Livonian, and the last native speaker of the Livonian language, Grizelda Kristina, died in Canada in 2013. Livonia and its culture's deterritorialisation has certainly been absolute.

An example rather closer to the geography of Mt Paektu and this book might be the attempt, as Korean nationalist historiography has it, of Imperial Japan and its colonial institutions between 1910 and 1945 to absolutely deterritorialise Korean culture and national identity by eradicating the Korean language and demanding the adoption of a new Imperial subjectivity by its colonial subjects. It is also, of course, of vital interest to North Korean historiography because Korean survival through this deterritorialising process is one of the key poles on which North Korean politics is founded. So relative deterritorialisation is of most interest to this chapter and to the consideration of North Korean politics and practices connected to it.

This chapter therefore focuses on what I claim to be a new invented tradition of North Korea, closely connected to the foundational mythology of Mt Paektu: a series of annual marches which are connected to the journeys and crossings of Kim Il Sung and Kim Jong Suk. Such journeys, as noted previously, contain the charismatic political energy from which the leadership and government of contemporary North Korea draw strength. This charisma is transmitted across time and into our and the North Korean present by not just the processes of scale and scaling mentioned above, but also through these relative processes of de- and reterritorialisation familiar to Deleuze and Guattari. The power of these journeys, crossings and charismatic moments is deterritorialised, abstracted and extracted from its original temporary and geographical context in the northern Korean peninsula of the 1930s and reterritorialised in our and North Korea's present in the guise of the performative invented traditions described by this chapter. While Deleuze and Guattari did not originally include a temporal frame in their writing, doing so here, so that such transformations also include detemporalisations and retemporalisations, allows for a more holistic consideration of the practices and implications of Pyongyang's new invented traditions.

In order to better ground the complex narratives of history and memory required to underpin Pyongyang's institutional power, constructed and invented traditions have been required. It is natural that a large number of these traditions revolve around the birthdays, moments of transition and triumph, or other important days in the lives of its dynastic leadership (Gabroussenko 2010). Another book chapter or indeed a whole book could perhaps focus on the invented traditions around the visits of one of the Kim family to factories, farms, hospitals and other institutions or pieces of infrastructure, which lead to these places being named after the day on which either Kim Il Sung or Kim Jong Il first visited them (Winstanley-Chesters 2015). A recent particular example of this tendency involved the centenary of the birth of Kim Jong Suk on 24 December 2017. While she already has a number of places named after her (such as Pyongyang's Kim Jong Suk Textile Mill), December 2017 saw many public events focused on both remembering her life, developing public interest in her narrative and embedding it in the minds of future generations. These events appeared to be a collaboration between central government, the Socialist Women's Union of Korea and the Korean Children's Union. Therefore, alongside the traditional wreath-laying ceremony at the Revolutionary Martyrs Cemetery (KCNA 2017a), the schoolchildren of Hoeryong watched and took part in a concert entitled "Eternal Sunray of Loyalty" at Hoeryong's Schoolchildren's Palace (KCNA 2017b). North

Korea's Central News Agency (KCNA), asserted that interest in her and sites connected to her was "steadily increasing", with some 300,000 visitors to Hoeryong in 2017 alone (KCNA 2017c). North Korea's central bank printed gold and silver coinage with an image of her childhood home (KCNA 2017d), and the Ministry of Railways put on display a railway carriage and velocipede (a hand-powered railway vehicle) that Kim Jong Suk had used in 1945 just after her return and the Liberation of Korea (KCNA 2017e). The crossings this chapter considers in detail have also been matched with events reterritorialising Kim Jong Suk's own moments of crossing. Important moments of historical memory essentially serve as North Korean 'saints' days', temporalisations and crystallisations of the supra-temporal and esoteric streams of narrative charisma. As well as a mythology, such events require a mythography onto which traditions and imagination can be implanted. While the developing mythology of the North Korean political present has been considered by past academic work (Kwon 2013), and even the structural elements of the mythography onto which it is laid (Joinau 2014), what has not been addressed is the developing tendency for North Korea to provide opportunities and spaces for its citizens to encounter for themselves the narrative and charismatic energies transmitted by these deterritorialisings and detemporalisings of important characters in the nation's history, such as our goddess of Mt Paektu, and to walk theatrically in the footsteps of the nationalist past. In doing so these citizens become actors and agents within the process of new invented traditions which seek to revivify the political energy of the past, bringing it physically into the present.

Far from Pyongyang and the current centres of political power and energy in North Korea, as well as the monolithic, commemorative architectures of the city, the Tuman and Amnok rivers on the nation's northern boundary, like Mt Paektu, play a huge role in the way the rest of the world conceives of the nation. Gazing across the rivers from China, foreign eyes see a landscape of deprivation, barren nature and failures in governmentality and development (Shim 2013). However, just like Mt Paektu these river boundaries have an enormous place in North Korea's own self-perception. Long considered the boundary between Korean national territory and that of either China or Manchuria, the Tuman and the Amnok and their shores play a vital role in the histories of North Korea and Korean nationalism as transition spaces or zones of malleability (Winstanley-Chesters 2016). Travel through or inter-action with these zones and spaces is in some Korean historical and mytho-logical memories akin to crossings in sacred literatures of other rivers such as the Styx or the Jordan, crossings which transform and transfigure the crosser (Havrelock 2011). Another aspect of such zones and places is that they are seen within both mythologies, histories and hagiographies as places in which 'special' or significant things are more likely or possible to happen than in other more conventional territory (Barthes 1972). New Testament Biblical texts even suggest that in such special places a special temporal frame exists in which *chronos* (χρόνος, chronological time) is replaced by *kairos* (καιρός, special/significant time) (Smith 1969).

Within North Korea's historiography the landscape of the Tuman and the Amnok is subject to an interesting historical dualism, in which the spaces of the rivers are both zones in which things that are significantly bad can happen and where events which are particularly positive can occur. In North Korea's historiography a number of key figures in the proto-North Korean nationalist guerrilla movements, such as Kim Il Sung and this book's 'goddess of Mt Paektu', Kim Jong Suk, have important moments of crossing and recrossing in their lives centred on these river zones (Winstanley-Chesters and Ten 2016). These important historical figures in North Korea's national story are forced by the circumstances of colonial rule to flee across the rivers to the less distinctly Imperial space of Manchuria (later Manchukuo). They later return in a no less transformative moment, crossing back over the rivers to begin their campaigns of guerrilla harassment of colonial forces, campaigns which of course later become foundational to North Korea's notion of revolution and sense of national self (Suh 1995). In the process of crossing, individuals such as Kim Il Sung and Kim Jong Suk not only support the transformation of the narrative of Korean or North Korean nationalism, but the transformation of their own selves. Connected via the transformative power of the de- and rematerialising process of crossing and recrossing into special or significant places and times, these important characters in North Korea's history are transfigured from their child or precarious lives as colonial subjects, to powerful resistive, aggressive, political adults (Winstanley-Chesters and Ten 2016). Kim Jong Suk in particular, as we have seen earlier in this book, was completely transfigured by her crossing, leaving as a slight child of oppressed and destitute sharecroppers and returning across the Tuman river as a politically aware, energetic expert in military tactics and excellent sniper.

Kim Jong Suk's husband, Kim Il Sung's own particular moment of river crossing, according to current North Korea historiography, occurred in January 1925 over the frozen waters of the Amnok River (Suh 1995). It was this crossing which in North Korean mythology begins the period of guerrilla exile from which so much of his authority and charisma in Pyongyang's conceptual mind derives. The year 2015 would be the ninetieth anniversary of this moment, so perhaps it should not be surprising that the event was marked. *Rodong Sinmun* on 23 January 2015 reported: "A national meeting took place at the People's Palace of Culture Wednesday to mark the ninetieth anniversary of the 250-mile journey for national liberation made by President Kim Il Sung" (Rodong Sinmun 2015a). Nor was it surprising that the newspaper continued its report with a paragraph of assertions:

> On January 22, Juche [Chuch'e] 14 (1925) Kim Il Sung started the 250-mile journey for national liberation from his native village Mangyongdae to the Northeastern area of China. During the journey he made up the firm will to save the country and the nation deprived by Japanese imperialism. New history of modern Korea began to advance along the unchangeable orbit of independence, Songun and socialism. (Rodong Sinmun 2015a)[42]

As is common in North Korean media, the text of the report attempts to include all three leaders produced by Pyongyang's political dynasty: the efforts of Kim Jong Il, the Dear Leader, to utilise this key source of nationalist power in 1975 through a commemorative march on its fiftieth anniversary is also addressed by the text. Finally space is also made for some of Kim Jong Un's rather urgent and vociferous Mt Paektu-focused themes found within 2015's New Year's Address:

> Respected Marshal Kim Jong Un is wisely leading the work to ensure that the sacred tradition of the Korean revolution started and victoriously advanced by Kim Il Sung and Kim Jong Il is given steady continuity [...] calling on the school youth and children to hold them in high esteem as the eternal sun of Juche and carry forward the march to Mt Paektu to the last. (Rodong Sinmun 2015a)

While repetition of past efforts and thoughts from North Korea's leadership might not be surprising in such a medium, the mention of the march is the first moment in which the invented tradition considered by this chapter appears. Observers and analysts of North Korean cultural and historical practice are familiar with many of the traditions connected to its political mythology. A good deal of them engage the audience and citizenry in worshipful, passive veneration of North Korea's political elite and their mythic past: standing in front of statues and monumental architectures, being shown sacred and important sites of memory, occasionally taking part in staged bouts of traditional dancing (Rodong Sinmun 2018a). So how would the school youth and children mentioned in the report from 2015 hold this 'sacred tradition' in esteem? By passive participation at a meeting of the Workers Party of Korea? Through the singing of songs and poems dedicated to moments of nationalist history recounted by the text? By appearing slightly overawed or afraid next to Kim Jong Un during a moment of on-the-spot-guidance? In fact the

---

[42] Emerging in the aftermath of Kim Il Sung's death in 1993, the ideological concept of 'Songun' is generally translated as 'military-first politics' and was deployed by North Korea's government during the period of extreme hardship (1994–98), during which Kim Jong Il stressed the importance of the army over the party as the principal organising state institution of the DPRK, and sought to mobilise the entire national population and all resources available for military purposes (Park 2007).

answer would be none of these things, but something far more important, something that worked apart and aside from North Korea's more conventional commemorative traditions. Instead of abstraction and narrative opacity, there would instead be a period of de- and reterritorialisation on the streets and paths of South Pyongan Province which itself would constitute a newly invented tradition. These schoolchildren would re-enact the crossing and journeys of Kim Il Sung in the 1930s, in the process using their own bodies as vessels and channels for the charismatic political energies rooted there for North Korean history. In short, by this rematerialisation of the political past the children themselves become Kim Il Sung and his small band of guerrillas.

There is a great deal missing in this first mention of this new tradition, much left out in the structure and conceptualisation, but this is not uncommon for North Korean political practices and praxis which often excludes content and coherence which might otherwise be expected. The process for the schoolchildren's selection, the nature of the institutions from which they came, their ages, the number of children involved, or even the exact length of the journey (as it is unclear whether the schoolchildren walk the entire distance) – elements which might support a really convincing re-enactment process elsewhere in the world and tie into political themes and agendas – are never stated within the *Rodong Sinmun* report of their enterprise. Yet the actual physicality and presence of their journey is clear and important to the narrative and the tradition. This physicality, common to pilgrimages elsewhere, in which breaks, pauses and stops must be taken, presumably in this case to rest the children's tired legs after having "crossed one steep pass after another", is clear to the reader and a real element in the construction of this event (Rodong Sinmun 2015b). These are presented as real children of North Korea in 2015, not simply cyphers for the pre-Liberation, nationalist past, revitalised by the ideological connection and charismatic energies of the history they re-enact.

Simply conceiving of this journey or pilgrimage as yet another theatrical moment in North Korea's ceaseless flow of historiography and hagiography, however, would be to miss some of the important elements of the process and fail to draw out the greater and deeper levels of context and connection which underpin this new tradition. The theatric or performative potential of the event is clear. The children pass through, in North Korean tradition and practice, a well-prepared and well-trodden list of charismatic terrains, a list that is no doubt ideologically and narratologically entirely sound. Having left Mangyongdae, Kim Il Sung's home village according to *Rodong Sinmun*'s report, the children on the first march passed Kaechon (South Pyongan Province), Kujang and Hyangsan (both North Pyongan Province), Huichon and Kangyye (Jagang), "along the historic road covered by the President with the lofty aim to save the destiny of the country and nation in the dark days when Korea was under the Japanese imperialists' colonial rule" (Rodong Sinmun 2015b)

Following Deleuze and Guattari's notion of deterritorialisation, the spaces of relation and the practices of relation within the frame of the schoolchildren's journey are equally as important as its starting point, route and destination, a fact held in common with much of the earlier narratives of North Korean journeying and crossing (Winstanley-Chesters 2015). Although within this newly invented tradition these children walk the route of the commemoration of what North Korea considers to be its period of national revolution and Liberation at this moment, temporally fixed in 2015, conceptually for those involved, however, it is supposed to be 1925. Whatever these North Korean children think in the quieter moments of their own particular everyday (perhaps watching South Korean TV dramas on smuggled in USB sticks, helping their parents engage in furtive transactions at semi-legal markets or coping with the mixed ennui of resignation, exasperation and desperation surely produced by daily interaction with Pyongyang's institutions), the social and personal context of those "dark days" in the late 1920s is activated and actualised by their every footstep. When they stopped for breaks they would hear the "impressions of the reminiscences of anti-Japanese guerrillas", and beginning their march again the schoolchildren, following the political power of those reminiscences, would become, represent, even channel the affect, relation and aspirations of those same guerrillas (Rodong Sinmun 2015b).

Following their departure from Pyongyang on 22 January 2015, these children arrived at their (and both Kim Il Sung and Kim Jong Il's) destination, Phophyong in Ryanggang Province, around 4 February (Rodong Sinmun 2015c). According to North Korean historiography, Phophyong is the actual site of Kim Il Sung's crossing of the Amnok river, the site where the young man would transition from subjugated Chosen (colonial-period Korea) and the political frame of colonisation, to resistance in the wild edges of Manchuria and new commitments and practices aiming for personal liberation and political and ideological struggle. This was the place and moment of Kim Il Sung's transformation and the foundational moment in this new invented tradition.

The North Korean historical narratives surrounding this book's 'new goddess of Mt Paektu', Kim Jong Suk, also, as this chapter has suggested and the reader will already have engaged with, have her leaving her home town of Hoeryong (North Hamgyong Province), and crossing the Amnok river in the early 1930s. In a similar way to that of Kim Il Sung, the crossing itself is conceived of as a moment of transformation, a harbinger of special times to come. It would not be surprising if other elements of this newly invented tradition of marching and rematerialisation would be used to repurpose and reconnect with the charismatic energies of Kim Jong Suk's crossing (Rodong Sinmun 2014).

There have since 2015 been a wide variety of periods in which groups of children, workers, civil servants and others within the institutional and political frameworks of North Korean society and bureaucracy engage in such walks, marches and study tours (Rodong Sinmun 2016, 2018b, 2020a–g), a number of which have marched and walked within some of the very same territory as the first march in 2015 (Rodong Sinmun 2018c). The Schoolchildren's March itself has been repeated again in 2016 and 2017 following a similar route, but with additions and subtractions on each occasion. Some have sought to connect other places and spaces of political memory and power into the routes of their walks and marches, still others have included museums and commemorative spaces themselves within the itinerary. The marching visit of the Korean Children's Union to Mangyongdae and the Youth Movement Museum in June 2018 serves as a good example of such walks (Rodong Sinmun 2018c). It would be possible to frame these as more conventional acts of pilgrimage, if they were not deeply integrated into the ecosystems of North Korean politics. There have even been connections with the rich history of sacred spaces on and around Mt Paektu, in particular to the Secret Guerrilla Camp, the bivouacs, cooking spaces and campsites of the guerrilla campaign, and even to the extraordinary 'slogan trees' (Rodong Sinmun 2018d). Paektusan's summit has not been excluded from these practices, and there have been a number of instances of study tours and marches of civil servants and bureaucrats visiting the peak of the mountain as part of their activities (Rodong Sinmun 2018d). While surely visits and ideological pilgrimages to the sacred spaces of political memory in North Korea are not a new element of its conceptual repertoire of practice, there is something distinctly new about this category of invented tradition.

There has been little in the way of extra development of the physical Schoolchildren's March since 2015. Although 2020's iteration appeared larger than the initial versions of the event in 2015 and 2016, *Rodong Sinmun*'s report of the start reads much the same (Rodong Sinmun 2020a). The Schoolchildren of 2020 began the march by holding a rally at Mangyongdae Revolutionary School in front of the statues of Kim Il Sung and Kim Jong Il. Choe Hwi, Vice Chair of the Workers Party of Korea's Central Committee, was present to see them off, and the route is described as being "Kaechon, Hyangsan and Kanggye to Phophyong", much the same as in earlier years (Rodong Sinmun 2020a). On 26 January, *Rodong Sinmun* reports that the Schoolchildren have reached and passed Hyangsan, visiting Kujang Inn, Chongchongang Ferry Revolutionary Site and Tokgol Revolutionary Site along the way and engaging in what the newspaper records as "diverse political and cultural work including presentation on the reminiscences of anti-Japanese guerrillas and a question-and-answer study" (Rodong Sinmun 2020b). As in 2015 and other previous years, they are met by party and local government officials at each point along the way and mark as many moments in the historical narratives of both Kim Il Sung's original march to Phophyong and Kim Jong Il's re-enactment of it (Rodong Sinmun 2020b). On 1 February 2020 *Rodong Sinmun* records the march's arrival in Kangyye, prior to which it had stopped at the Chongun and Pyolha inns and crossed the Myongmun and Kubong passes (Rodong Sinmun 2020c). Finally on, 4 February, as in previous years, *Rodong Sinmun* records the Schoolchildren's March has having arrived in Phophyong to be greeted once more by Choe Hwi (Rodong Sinmun 2020d), and as always, unlike Kim Il Sung, to not cross the Amnok river.

While the Schoolchildren's March may not differ greatly in 2020 from its first contemporary iteration in 2015, the slogans and uniforms (even down to the blue and red jumpsuits worn by participants) being highly similar, what is different is the fact that, far from being perhaps the only long-distance commemorative march or event at this time in the North Korean political year (after the oath-taking sessions traditionally following the New Year's Address and in 2020 following the Fifth Plenary Meeting), many other study tours now share the pages of *Rodong Sinmun* and feature on North Korean television. Such study tours are not infrequent across Pyongyang's ideological calendar, but in 2020 in particular there have been a number of tours from organisations such as the Union of Agricultural Workers of Korea (Rodong Sinmun 2020e), the Kimilsungist-Kimjongilist Youth League (Rodong Sinmun 2020f) and even the "Commanding officers of the Korean People's Internal Security Forces" (Rodong Sinmun 2020g) to the politically important sites around Mt Paektu. The year 2019 even saw the Schoolchildren's March displaced for a year by a study tour and visit to the important sites of Kim Jong Il's life to mark his seventy-seventh birthday anniversary (Rodong Sinmun 2019). So in one sense there has been little change to the Schoolchildren's March in form, content or geography when it appears, and there have often been study tours and pedagogic political moments in North Korea's recent history, but the business of the current schedule of such events does seem to be new. Reiteration of all manner of political, historical and ideological themes is perhaps at a premium towards the end of this first decade of Kim Jong Un's rule.

## Marching and Reterritorialising in 2015 and Beyond

The Schoolchildren's March of 2015 has been repeated in 2016, 2017, 2018 and again in 2020, so in the end was not simply a one off re-enactment to connect to the particular energies generated by that year, or by the at the time impending centenary in 2017 of the birth of this book's 'new goddess of Mt Paektu', Kim Jong Suk, who of course also engaged in river crossings and much journeying around the same time. These marches are also not commemo-rating one particular moment in the history of Kim Il Sung's journeys and crossings, because they do not follow a coherent or specific path of a single journey made by him. Instead as much as they reterritorialise collections of powerful moments, such as the crossings of the river, they are also assemblages of a number of different bits of historical narrative from the period within a geographical area generally considered to be charismatic within North Korea's political history and connected to Mt Paektu, which is certainly charismatic in not just North Korea's history, but across the cultural, spiritual and political histories of all iterations of the Korean nation. Essentially the march is a repertoire of important moments of historical memory connected together in such a way as to amplify the charismatic energies present within each moment.

However important and interesting the Schoolchildren's March may be, readers should not only think about the specific event in 2015 (just like specific moments in the whole historiography of Kim Jong Suk), but perhaps also consider movement, crossing, journeying and their utility and usefulness in North Korea to be processes of political scaling and rescaling. While such organised de- and reterritorialisings (and intrinsic de- and retemporalisings) are novel as newly invented traditions, Pyongyang's institutions have often harnessed the power of a particular sort of physical movement within its developmental and institutional strategies in order to underpin its goals or reconfigure the agenda. Analysts and watchers of North Korea will be familiar in recent years with the terms 'shock brigades' (ch'ungkyŏkyŏdan) and 'soldier builders' (pyŏngsa kŏnch'ukŏpja) (Rodong Sinmun 2018g) These categories of worker or operative are common to development of infrastructure projects in North Korea, deployed from an institutional network rooted in the Workers Party of Korea or the Korean People's Army either at moments of crisis for a pre-existing project or to undertake a key element of a new piece of strategy at an accelerated timescale. *Rodong Sinmun* and other North Korean media often report on the call for their usage or their later or finished work on the project. Often when these media do so they make sure to comment on the manner and rapidity of their journey to the site (Rodong Sinmun 2018g). It would surely not surprise the reader to hear that such journeys are often undertaken at considerable speed. The journeys of these 'shock brigades' and 'soldier builders' are themselves part of the theatric process of North Korean politics, just like the journeys of Kim Jong Suk. In the terminology of Geography, they are practical technologies of scale and scaling in which the political/social frames and praxis of the centre are rescaled elsewhere in the nation's landscape and embedded in new terrains, reconfiguring provincial or peripheral political/social frames as they do so (Winstanley-Chesters 2014). As might be familiar to Erik Swyngedouw, such processes have most recently been seen within North Korea's hydrological and hydro-power industries, as the energy and authority of the state has been brought to bear on the river and reservoir systems of the country, embedding the logics and agenda of a particular form of politics in that terrain (Swyngedouw 2015). The invented traditions of the

Schoolchildren's March and other marches or practices of journeying are themselves scalar processes in common with these pre-existing traditions.

Beyond North Korea's more conventional and historically familiar efforts to scale and rescale its political energies across its territory, the journeys reconfigured within the newly invented traditions which this chapter encounters and explores are in themselves also acts of rescaling. However, more than the practices and processes of aligning the agenda of the periphery, such as North Korea's more remote provinces of Ryanggang and Chagang, to the political aspirations of the centre of power in Pyongyang, these traditions scale through and across time. Coupled with the processes of de- and reterritorialisation and de- and retemporalisation, the schoolchildren participants interact with the powerful political energies of North Korea's mythological or historiographic past (the charisma on which the (perceived) authority and legitimacy of Pyongyang's Paektusan Generals and Kim Jong Suk sit), rescaling it into the present day and our own temporal plane. These marches, processes and journeys are themselves therefore scalar acts, as much as they are invented traditions. In the practice and process of these acts the participants are conceived of as not just re-enacting the journeys and travels of the past, as cyphers and metaphorical vessels for them, but in some way they are transfigured into the physical realities of those charismatic figures and the goddess who once, in North Korea's historical imagery, trod the same paths and ground around these spaces of crossing, Mt Paektu and elsewhere.

## CHAPTER SEVEN

# Korean Mountains and Modern Asceticism

Moving on from the historiographies and invented traditions of this book's 'new goddess of Mt Paektu' and more recent developments in North Korea, this penultimate chapter of the book seeks to both move back to the mountainous terrain so familiar in the rest of the text, but also to consider new mountain practices elsewhere in Korea and beyond the narratives of Kim Jong Suk. While these stories of Kim Jong Suk, mountain immortals and the charismatic revolutionaries of North Korean history (as much of the country's cultural and political practice can) make the nation appear a little unique, aberrant or an outlier compared with the wider world, it is vital to understand that this is not entirely the case. When it comes mountain practices, mountain narratives and transforming cultural terrains, North Korea is not unique, and so this chapter is an effort to engage with South Korea and developments in mountain practice and engagement there.

Contemporary South Korea, as previously suggested by this book, appears at first sight to be radically different from the culture which produced its traditional mountain practices. However, deeper analysis of Korean society shows that some of these traditions are not abandoned and in fact some continue almost unchanged since more ancient times. Further to this, still many other mountain traditions are reshaped by the prerogatives of contemporary economics and social development. Korean history is marked by these traditions, and also by the practical and logistical impact of the peninsula's topography. The mountains of Korea were both a protector against external forces and a drag on bureaucratic or economic exchange. The dramatic landscapes of the peninsula made travelling along or across it difficult, made the exchange of goods and resources throughout the nation impractical, resulting in a real impact on the geospatial awareness of its citizens. Modernity does more than just flatten politics and economics, it flattens time and geospatiality. Technology and economic development began to make an impact in the later stages of the Yi dynasty and this only continued later during the Japanese colonial period.

A key element of that impact was the transformation of spatial connections across the nation through the building of railways and roads. Korean towns, villages and provinces were brought much closer together. Once impassable and treacherous mountains and wildernesses were made accessible and bridged by the infrastructures of modernity. This transformation of spatial awareness and connectivity brought about a new ascetic and aesthetic sensibility upon the mountains of Korea, a sensibility also directly tied to new forms of social and economic organisation. Yet there is a friction at the very heart of this development: Korean mountain traditions have lived long in the body of the peninsula, and are of course not about to yield easily.

This chapter therefore explores the routes of these new ascetic and aesthetic forms as they connect to South Korean mountains, tracing them from formative moments in the forge of colonialism and imperialism to their appropriation in the context of East Asian imperial politics. These forms produced new categories of mountain practice which are now familiar throughout the globe, but which were once innovative, new and shocking. These new forms held radically different aesthetic sensibilities which have produced new landscapes in mountains in many different nations. These sensibilities and practices include the culture of hiking and mountain climbing so common around South Korean urban centres. New technologies of travel, such as the network of KTX high-speed railway lines, help to develop such endeavours. To better understand such topography in the modern age it will be necessary to move briefly away from the Korean peninsula to Europe, the historical engine for technological, economic and cultural transformation which produced the colonial and post-colonial world of consumption and capitalism that so marks the globe in the twenty-first century.

Within this book we have encountered East Asian and Korean mountain traditions which to external eyes and ears may seem esoteric as much as they are mythological. The historical roots of mountain worship and mountain practice in European traditions might be distant and in most cases lost, but they are as remarkable in many cases as those of Asia. From the Huldufólk ('hidden people', i.e. trolls and Jötnar [giants]) of Iceland and other Scandinavian nations, embedded deeply in their mountains, rocks and wilderness landscapes (Árnason 1972; Simpson 1978), to Central European traditions such as those of the Magyar (modern-day Hungarians), rooted in multidimensionality in which forests and mountains play significant spiritual roles, wilderness topographies (Róna-Tas 1999) form key parts of historical European mythographies. The UK, a vital locus of Enlightenment rationalism and progenitor of much of the philosophy of capitalism which has driven recent changes in mountain culture across the globe, has historical mythologies of a similarly esoteric nature. British mountain places are particularly marked by mythologies which have come to underpin the nation's contemporary nationalism, such as those of Arthurian legend (Dixon-Kennedy 2005). However, the islands' mountains have also been influenced by Nordic and Celtic mythologies which have left residual memories of cosmic forces and mythic creatures, such as dragons, trolls and witches. A number of mountains and hills across the country are recounted within these mythologies to be the resting sites or properties of dragons, such as Cnoc na-Cnoimh ('worm's hill' in Gaelic, worm being a reference to dragons or the Devil's worms), in Sutherland, northern Scotland, which was protected by a very jealous and violent dragon (Simpson 1978). Others, such as Caer Caradoc in the county of Shropshire, are themselves reputed to be sleeping, dormant or transformed dragons (Simpson 1978). Still other mountains are remembered in mythology as having been generated by the actions of giants. Cadair Idris, for example, one of the highest mountains in Wales, is recorded as the throne of one of that nation's semi-mythic giant kings, Idris Gawr (Idris the Giant), who in the sixth century CE used the mountain as a seat to gaze over his whole mountainous kingdom of Merionnydd (Williams 1860).

Of course this rich mythic topography has been no protection against the contemporary radical reconfiguration of mountain traditions. The majority of this mythology and its landscapes have been lost to the cultural and national memories of those nations. Accordingly in Europe and the West, veneration of mountainous spaces entered contemporary consciousness through the tendencies of artists and poets to resist or counter modernity, but not to connect with these more ancient mythologies and mythographies.

The ascent of peaks would be conjoined in nineteenth-century Britain as both romantic encounter with nature, and masculine conquering of challenging terrain by the middle- or upper-class man.[43] The accumulation of wealth and extraction of labour value from the newly urban workers allowed the man of leisure a more sedentary life. This life could be made more authentic through

---

[43] Mountain spaces such as the Lake District in England were popularised and transformed in the public imagination of Imperial Britain by romantic artists and writers. Thomas Gray's 1769 account of his grand tour of the Lake District was but the first writing to reconfigure the once peripheral and underdeveloped landscape of mountains, moors and lakes. Before long the romantic poetry of Wordsworth, Coleridge and Southey, along with the paintings of the Cooper brothers and the philosophy and craft of John Ruskin, would entice countless gentlemen of leisure, and later with the coming of the railways, the working classes, to imagine the area as an athletic and cultural utopia. This process of intersection between culture, imperial logics, leisure and upland spaces would be reproduced across the British Empire and beyond. It would find its ultimate conclusion in the conquest of Mt Everest and heroic failures in Antarctica by gentlemen amateurs. Hill walking, fell running and rambling would all become key activities in these landscapes, in part supported by mapping technology in Britain derived from military efforts during the Napoleonic Wars of the turn of the nineteenth century.

the adoption of energetic, challenging exercise such as mountain climbing and hillwalking (Bailey 1978).[44]

This landscape of commerce, commodification and conquering is nowadays familiar to climbers and mountaineers of East Asia as well. The infrastructures that greet those who wish to ascend Mt Fuji or other Japanese mountains, or Mt Sorak and Mt Suri in Korea, would be familiar to hillwalkers across the globe (Dax 2015). The aesthetic and ascetic of mountain practices in our age are both key products and drivers of globalisation in these mountains. Mountains as places of leisure are interwoven with political and economic modernity; walking in mountains becomes defined and limited by the speed of modernity and globality. Tourists and visitors to the mountains have thus to return back to the city according to the rigours and strictures of the public transport schedule. There must be food and services on the mountains to meet the needs of these modern pilgrims, along with opportunities for the consumption of products through which they encounter the mountain spaces, such as walking sticks, expensive clothing, GPS and satellite orientation equipment. These facilities and infrastructures in a way act as amplifiers for globalisation and capitalism on the mountains, drawing both topography and pilgrims into their logic. The chapters of this book have so far encountered mountain practices on the Korean peninsula. We now move to Japan, a vital site of mountain tradition, and at one point a coloniser of the Korean peninsula. Japan is Korea's neighbour, and a very useful example of mountain practice, both in history and in the present.

Japan is a highly developed nation, one of the most technologically advanced in the world. The landscape of larger islands such as Honshu and Hokkaido is an extraordinary product of modernity, criss-crossed by high speed Shinkansen railway lines and towns built according to an architecture of extremely high density. Japanese society is equally famed for its rigorous submission to the cultural-economic milieu generated by this terrain. Contemporary practices of hillwalking in Japan are also famous for their binding into the logics of consumerism, the landscapes accessible by complex public transport arrangements and well served by impressive collections of food and catering facilities.

The Ainu or Ezo (蝦夷) who had once inhabited Aomori Province, at the far north of the Japanese main island Honshu, were exterminated from the area by the middle of the eighteenth century but have left extensive cultural traces among its mountains. The area's mountains are renowned for their history of geological shift and volcanism, which have produced a rugged landscape deeply affective to cultural traditions. The Nebuta festivals in Aomori and Hirosaki cities serve as a ritualisation of a ninth-century military victory by

---

[44] In a similar way, the economic rise of the 1980s contributed to the development of hiking culture in South Korea.

General Tamuramaro over the Ainu. Enormous floats replete with lanterns in the shape of demonic characters, once important in Ainu culture, are key elements in the festival. The story of General Tamuramaro's victory over Ainu has a connection to Mt Iwaki (岩木山), which was a very active volcano during the last millennium and has its explosive history memorialised in local traditions.

One side of Mt Iwaki, known as Akakura, is described as the location of interaction between immortals, an ancient marriage between an indigenous female divinity and a foreign male conqueror (Schattschneider 2003, 33). The Dragon Princess resident at Mt Iwaki gave the deity Utsushikunitama a precious stone as a confirmation of their union. However, traditional Edo texts replaced Utsushikunitama with a living official, General Tamuramaro, asserting that their marriage symbolises the new power of Yamato Japanese culture over Ainu. This marriage is now commemorated in the Akakura mountain shrine by praxis, artistic production and architecture (Schattschneider 2003, 34).

Akakura and its shrine architectures are at first glance a product of spiritual and cultural history, yet they are tinged with political change. Similarly, the landscape of Mt Paektu examined in this book is deeply ingrained with the political energy of North Korea. Readers will have seen that the architectures of North Korea's political memory at Mt Paektu dramatically influence the ascetic practices of those who seek interaction with its topography, both historically and in the present day. Likewise memories are projected upon Akakura's slopes and the immortals enshrined there. An elaborate ecosystem of ritual has been bestowed on Akakura following a revival of practice upon the mountain in the 1920s. A number of mediums and sages recount spiritual visitations from Akakura deities, and the congregation of Akakura's shrine maintain complicated traditions (Schattschneider 2003, 50).

Akakura mountain is believed to be particularly important for women's health and well-being. For generations women have conceived of Akakura's topography as therapeutic and revelatory, visiting the shrines at the base of Akakura to pray for fertility and childbirth, and further up the mountain they activate their inner 'heat' in order to triumph over mortal ills (Schattschneider 2003, 65). This may remind us of *tapas*, the magical Indian tradition which was later absorbed by yoga practices. *Tapas* means 'heat', 'ardour' or 'zeal' and indicates ascetical austerities in general, and one tantra-yoga practice consists of generating inner warmth ('mystical heat') in the body (Eliade 1969, 106–8).

Moving then to the intersection of ascetic practice and mountain traditions in South Korea, Jongheon Jin gives a useful analysis of the transformations of mountain landscape, ascetic practice and ancient traditions within the developing social terrain. One such ascetic was Huh Man-soo, who was even nicknamed 'Mt Chirisan Immortal'. While living in Japan he had been heavily influenced by the modern mountain leisure practices there and become a keen mountain climber. Having returned to Korea he abandoned his family and lived as a hermit in a mud hut on the slopes of Chirisan. As a mountain immortal, he was one of those who took part in building modern Korean mountain asceticism. In Huh's hands, Mt Chiri would be a terrain for leisure, as he made the first hiking maps of the area, erected signage and "rescued many people who were wounded, exhausted, or lost in the mountains" (Jongheon 2005). This person was active in the co-production of new mountain places, connected to civic mores and a developing democratic and consumptive asceticism. In this regard, Huh was very much a part of a modern South Korea (Jongheon 2005).

Huh Man-soo deeply loved Mt Chiri in his later life; this mountain influenced his sense of self and agency, even to the moment of his disappearance somewhere on the mountain in June 1976. This motif of the disappearance into the mountains of a person who dedicated to them his life clearly echoes the tendency of Korean traditional *sanshin* mentioned in Chapter Three, where merging with a mountain was one of the ways to become a mountain god or immortal. Against the background of the modern Korea of democracy, civic organisation, functional bureaucracy and consumption, the new ascetic generated by Huh fulfilled a need for present-day immortals. Due to institutional changes that would generate South Korea's first national parks in 1987, Mt Chiri's shelters, once inhabited by Huh Man-soo, would fall under the control of the Korean National Parks Authority. There is a layering of older traditions of mountain immortals and contemporary practices of social engagement over Korean mountains which coexist with each other in creative collaboration. The new mountain topographies produced by political and economic modernity such as Mt Chiri are entwined in new nationalism, their power and ancient authority projected onto new landscapes. Together with this new political formation involving mountainous spaces, the social mores of Korean society moved on, driven by the developing imperatives of capital and consumption.

South Korea in the 1980s saw a large growth in hiking, coinciding with the rise of leisure culture and *sŏngin undong* (成人運動, sports for adults). The popularity of these practices was made possible by the thriving economy of the time, which contributed to the development of a middle class with sufficient means to fund self-perfection in the industrial setting (Dax 2015, 83). In this way mountain culture and hiking were reinvented in a new context, serving to counterbalance urbanisation (Dax 2015).

Urbanisation, commodification and the swift development of transport infrastructure have produced enormous pressures on Korean environmental and social landscapes. However, there is a character who, almost in response to these pressures, connects contemporary mountain ascetics and aesthetics with the traditional mountain culture of Korea. The KTX high-speed railway network is one of South Korea's most celebrated infrastructural achieve-ments. Its construction in the early 2000s threatened to flatten time across the peninsula, and to flatten and eradicate many of the mountainous spaces along its route. Mt Cheonseong in South Gyeongsang Province was it seems blessed with extraordinary luck that it should be the home of Jiyul Sŭnim.[45] Jiyul is a Buddhist nun based at the Naewon-sa monastery on Mt Cheonseong. When the mountain fell in the way of the KTX construction project, she undertook a series of protests that would serve as a challenge to South Korean develop-mental institutions. She later was treated by her supporters and opponents as something of a modern Korean priestess to a mountain god, or even *sanshin* herself:

> For some strange reason, I began to shed tears, tears that did not cease. I felt that the mountain was crying; I heard its pleas, begging for its life. These pleas moved me to promise the mountain that I would help. (Jiyul Sunim quoted in Cho 2013)

Jiyul raised awareness of the desecration of the mountain through sit-ins, prostrations, hunger strikes and finally a court case on behalf of a particular species of salamander whose habitat would be destroyed by construction. Although ultimately unsuccessful, as the tunnel was built and KTX trains now run at speed underneath the mountain, Jiyul nevertheless exploded the imperatives of contemporary ecological development and environmental consciousness. It appears that it was Jiyul's Korean Buddhist traditions which spurred her awareness of the unity and mutuality of all beings. Eun-so Cho suggests that Jiyul drew from the Buddhist concept of the interconnectedness of beings, described as dependent origination, an understanding that nothing exists independently of other things. In Jiyun's mind she and other living beings are at one not only with the inhabitants of the ecosystem which she sought to protect, but with the landscape itself (Cho 2013). Incorporation of the life of a mountain into a political protest made Jiyul a powerful figure in public life, and the image of her as a modern mountain immortal was created by a public and press, confused, hostile or inspired by her actions. This image suggests that new forms of mountain culture, new Korean mountain goddesses, may yet be generated in future, a process which will happen in its own time and on its own terms.

Since ancient times Koreans have believed that mountains are alive and should be communicated with, respected and worshipped. In contemporary times this East Asian understanding of the universe as living and sentient has been termed by Jane Bennett as "vibrant matter" (Bennett 2010). A great many

---

[45]  *Sŭnim* (스님) means a Buddhist monk or nun in Korean, while *nim* (님) is a honorific suffix.

spiritual traditions across the globe hold to concepts that the earth and things and beings on it are all alive. They live, breath, are active and energetic. On the Korean peninsula the traditions of *sanshin* and *sinsŏn* embody spiritual notions vital to the people who live there. However, on the contemporary Korean peninsula the agencies of the state think nothing of driving a tunnel miles through a sacred mountain, smashing its rock and degrading its ecosystem for the sake of progress. This is the violence and transformation enacted by the logics of capital and modernity upon the landscapes of the nation, in spite of whatever traditions may lay beneath or alongside the non-human or more than human. Jiyul's campaigns, through their peacefulness and connection with past traditions, lay this violence abundantly clear. This transformative power of her mountain practice is essentially the point of connection between her and the other actors in this book.

In the following and concluding chapter I attempt to harness the power of these connections to revisit the key themes of the book. I aim to connect transformations, mythologies, moments of violence and the gendering of the landscapes of nature and narrative to reiterate some of the most important elements. However, just as Jiyul's campaigns of protest against the obliteration of her landscape suggest new processes at work within these ancient thematic structures and webs, in the final section of this book I do hope to trace some of the potential of such processes within the landscapes of the myths I have been most concerned with. North Korean politics and its commemorative practices are social-cultural terrains on the move, constantly reconfiguring themselves, as much as they seek to maintain authority and connection with the past. Transformative and mythic histories are in active dialectic with the past.

## CHAPTER EIGHT

# Conclusion

Readers will have by now met this book's new goddess and many other characters who are both transformed by and transformative of Mt Paektu and other Korean mountains. While for the majority of this book I focused on Kim Jong Suk and her transformations, Chapter Six sought to connect to more recent invented traditions in North Korea and Chapter Seven introduced a selection of more recent interlocutors with the peninsula's mountains. Kim Jong Suk's narrative and these many other characters and traditions harness ancient spiritual energies inherited by contemporary Korean culture, but they also reflect new developments on the peninsula. In this Kim Jong Suk connects with the characters the reader will have met in the previous chapter, Jiyul Sŭnim and Huh Man-soo. All demonstrate examples of contemporary mountain practice, responding to the pressures of modern political, social and economic life in Korea.

Where has the reader been in this book? One particular mountain. Paektu and its role in the history and culture of both contemporary Korean nations was explored in Chapter Two. Mt Paektu's place within Korean historiography and developing modern nationalisms on the peninsula suggests a monolithic topography. Such a landscape could certainly provide abundant space for transformation not only of individuals but of nation and history. Traditions surrounding the place and role of the Tan'gun and genesis myths of the Korean nation and kingship would provide the foundation for such transformations. This chapter considered those traditions more generally in Korea, but also in the development of North Korean nationalism and statehood.

Traditions of transformation and spiritual power require fertile cultural ground from which to spring. Chapter Three therefore considered the roots which enable transformation within the wider framework of Korean cultural tradition. The reader will have encountered in this chapter traditions of Korean mountain deities such as *sanshin* and *sinsŏn*, their worship and the importance of mountainscapes and uplands. Such Korean mountain traditions have a great deal of potential energy; power which can well be used for the transformations in this book. The concept of *Paektu-taegan*, in which Korea is a topographic ecosystem of lines of sacred energy transmission across the territory of the peninsula, powers these transformations. Similarly traditions powered by *Paektu-taegan* project themselves through the practices of contemporary *sŏndo* culture. This culture further embeds itself in Korean sensibilities through the artistic and creative use of both mountains and mountain deities. Of great importance to this book are those cultural productions which construct female and feminine divine images.

Moving further than the contextualisation of Korean mountain cultures, mountain practices and transformative energies, the reader will have encountered specific characters and traditions. In common with contemporary Koreans who seek to harness the power of redeveloped and reconfigured mountain practices to transform their own lives, residents and citizens of the peninsula across history been subject to political and sociocultural transformation. During the late nineteenth century and colonial periods, what it was to be a Korean, and indeed what Korea was in the context of colonialism, unequal treaties and great powers, changes. Those who sought to resist colonial and Imperial power from Japan, doing so through the frame of Marxist and class analysis, would go on ultimately to form the first political elites and leaders of North Korea. Today North Korean politics, culture and history is tied intricately to the family of Kim Il Sung. Chapter Four not only rooted itself in that narrative, but in the external academic, theoretical framing which considers North Korea's place in global politics and culture. The chapter analysed the transformations of a young Kim Jong Suk, doing so with the narratives of Korean mountain culture and mountain spirit worship in mind, as well as knowledge of contemporary North Korean history, culture and politics. These transformations focus on the structural violence of her childhood through to her political awakening and transformation through education. Chapter Five then moved her narrative on to the period in which Kim Jong Suk is transformed in the landscapes of the north of the peninsula, in particular around and on Mt Paektu. Through her transformations within North Korea's narrative Kim Jong Suk becomes a mountain immortal. This is the case not just for her own lifespan in conjunction with the sacred topographies in which she is active, but, at least in the North Korean ideological mind, for all time.

In Chapter Six the book moved beyond the narratives of Kim Jong Suk, but not beyond North Korea, to consider recent invented traditions which connect to transformations wrought by space and place, and in particular the crossings and recrossings of that nation's historical past and the contemporary re-enactments such as the Schoolchildren's March. In Chapter Seven the book went geographically and conceptually further and considered transformative traditions elsewhere in East Asia, such as the Asakura tradition in Japan, where the reader will have encountered other narratives of co-production between mountain and people which are embedded in each other. Bringing these co-productions up to the present the chapter encounters transformations in near contemporary Korea in the mountain practices of Huh Man-soo and Jiyul Sŭnim. Both continue the traditions articulated by the new goddess and this book, of intersections between personal and landscape transformations.

Throughout the whole of this book and its many mythologies, mythographies and legendary traditions, I use a Foucauldian frame to consider the new goddess, Kim Jong Suk, and her self-transformations as technologies of self. These technologies are both applied by the goddess of this book and by the writers of the narratives and myths in which they are included. Technologies of the self are conventionally understood as personal and self-transformative technologies and practices deployed directly at the individual level, but in this book they are used in a much more comprehensive and wide-ranging manner. In the North Korean mythologies the reader will have encountered in this book, many technologies are deployed on the participants in the narratives. Kim Jong Suk herself uses education and educative practices as a technology of the self. She uses education to transform herself from an oppressed child to a fully fledged revolutionary fighter. She herself uses technologies of the self to develop other fighters and characters in her own mythology. She inculcates the weak and uneducated to become strong and ideologically worthy. Together her band of female guerrillas are seen deploying practical transformative techniques to underpin their roles and capabilities in the field. When the political and liberation struggles are over in 1945, Kim Jong Suk is transformed again into a different form of immortal for North Korean politics. Her own motherhood is used as a technological aspect in the history of the nation, the mother of the revolution, of its second and future generations. In the narratives not only is victory given to her in a manner transformative to her own self, but degrading violence done to her is also used to transform her. Violence enacted on others by her in the mythologies is also transformative, but is, as the reader will have seen, a co-production with the landscapes in which she experiences combat. These co-produced spaces are in tandem with the narratives used in North Korean history and commemorative practice, technologies in which to embed its current population. North Koreans can utilise the technologies of the self as demonstrated by Kim Jong Suk, and these technologies are deployable at different temporal moments, in the past, present and future. In contemporary North Korea the moments and landscapes of Kim Jong Suk's self-transformations and technologies of self are themselves technologies. Her places of violence, places of care, places of education are part of North Korea's commemorative and memorial architectures.

These technologies of self and self-transformations hark back to practices of the subtle body, as much as they do to ancient traditions of East Asian alchemy and powerful memories of Korean *sanshin* and Asian immortality.

In this they are rooted deeply in the cultural memories of East Asia and their various physical manifestations in the landscapes of its various nations. At the same time these landscapes are deeply important to the development of modern Asian nationalisms. This is not a new development, as we have seen Japanese examples in which half-remembered victories over precursors to Japanese homogeneity are commemorated in tandem with mountain landscapes and wild places in the north of Honshu. Mt Paektu, the mountain essential to the narratives of the new goddess of this book, is just such a place. Once peripheral to Korea, beyond its national boundaries, Mt Paektu has been reconfigured from the mythic past of the Tan'gun and other Korean deities to a fundamental element of modern Korean national self-identity. Mt Paektu is a vital piece of North Korean technology of the national self, demonstrated in this book through the co-productions of resistance on its slopes. However, it is also important to South Korea and to inter-Korean relations. In the period of Korean reconciliation in 2018, Mt Paektu was present in interactions between Moon Jae-in and Kim Jong Un, when soil from Mt Paektu was mixed with soil from Mt Halla on Jeju (as well as water from the Taedong and Han rivers), in a quasi-shamanistic act of territorial unification.

This book's goddess acts on and is acted on by the landscapes and terrains into which her mythologies are written. In this way her narratives and technologies become co-productions with the mountainous spaces themselves. As her stories revolve around one particular mountain, this book has considered Mt Paektu as a character in its own right. It is an active participant in a way that Debarbieux and Rudaz have considered it possible for upland places to become completely enmeshed in human cultures. Even when Mt Paektu was not even technically part of Korea, it served a bounding role within the conceptualisation of Korean national territory. In the mind of the colonial adventurers encountering Korea and Asia for the first time in the nineteenth century, Mt Paektu was recounted as being large beyond its actual physical size to a truly monolithic scale. It has been reimagined as a mountain anew in the present. The energies and authorities produced on and around the mountain are, as Erik Swyngedouw would understand it, rescaled throughout Korea's space and time. While no techno-natures are built upon its slopes, North Korea has constructed architectures and monuments upon and near the mountain which might constitute an ideologic-nature. Here through the memories of the goddess Kim Jong Suk and others, history and mythology are written anew on the area's physical topography.

Mt Paektu and the landscapes of Kim Jong Suk, its new goddess, are transformed into what Castree, Cosgrove and other scholars would conceive of as political or symbolic nature. The book has talked about North Korea's charismatic politics and ideology in the present, and how its contemporary ideology transforms all within the nation into performers on the political stage.

This stage, however, in North Korea also has no bounds. It is thus extended out into the physical terrain of the nation, becoming a charismatic landscape. Such a landscape is made of active, energetic vibrant matters which play and perform within the lifespans and mythologies of their narratives, and these lively materials contribute to the charisma of the politics embedded within them. The boulders which protect Kim Jong Suk from harm, the trees from which she does others fatal injury, the trees on which Kim Jong Suk's signature is wrought and from which the cabin in which she gives birth to Kim Jong Il is made all are within the web of charisma. All of them are vibrant as Jane Bennett and Sarah Whatmore would understand, possessed of their own agency, but also generating energy and agency for the mythologies and histories which they underpin and for North Korea's charismatic politics. In the process of supporting the new goddess to become an immortal herself, the landscape of Mt Paektu and its surroundings itself becomes immortal, just as the ideology of North Korea also aims to become.

This immortality across all the bounds of time and space is as much an invented tradition as it is one currently still in process and under production. Whether Kim Jong Suk and her fellow female guerrillas will be historical figures of power and importance in decades to come is debatable. Whether even Mt Paektu continues to develop in significance and accrue greater cultural and national energies, or whether it takes another new form in years to come, is impossible to know. In part all of these traditions are invented, but that does not stop them being powerful and does not stop them being useful in present and future. They are invented with a great many of the traditions and mythologies of the Korean peninsula and elsewhere, including ideas and frames of modern nationalism. It is precisely because they are caught in a network of invented traditions, imagined communities and cultural productions that the new goddess of the book and the landscape with which she engages are so useful to North Korea, and that the other contemporary traditions recounted by this book prove so useful in South Korea.

What, however, if North and South Korea no longer exist? What if there is at some point in the future only one Korea? Many readers will perhaps say that in fact there has only ever been one Korea and that the current status quo as far as sovereignty is concerned is a glitch or an aberration generated by the outworking of colonialism and the Cold War. While the author expects this book to be read for many years and decades to come and so it is important to make it as timeless as possible, the moment in which some of the material about these invented traditions was written seemed quite special, as 2018 saw an unexpected rapprochement between the two Koreas and across the landscape this book is concerned with. The writing of this book is therefore in a sense a work of mythological unification. It has attempted to unite traditions from across the peninsula, and united them in acts of self-transformation in one of the places most important to the Korean national self. Readers might want to consider the role or place of such unifications in the future, during a moment of concrete unification on the peninsula.

How might Kim Jong Suk be commemorated, remembered or mythologised in a time period in which some of the politics and ideology which birthed her disappears or is transformed? Readers will perhaps easily consider this in relation to Kim Jong Suk, given that the hegemony of Capitalism and Democracy, a transformation of South Korea's cultural-economic system to be more like North Korea, would be hard to imagine. Kim Jong Suk is in a sense already confined to the past, confined to memory. North Korea's use of her as a technology of self as much as an invented tradition harnesses this fact. It makes her memory and her body malleable, pliable and scalable in the present. As might be suggested, the new goddess Kim Jong Suk, like many aspects of North Korean ideology and politics, is powerful partly because she can be anything that Pyongyang needs her to be. But how will her memory and her transformations and technologies be used in a future with no North Korea, or with a unified Korea? Would unification diminish Kim Jong Suk? Would her powerful technologies, her subtle body, her energy and memory be forgotten or negated?

In these essentially unanswerable questions are the limits of this book. The key point for the author is the living nature of Kim Jong Suk, her vibrancy and energy in the present narratives and traditions of the communities and nations served by them. While they are a great distance in the past and mythic in tone, they are still accessible through the practices, narrative techniques and technologies of self I have described in this book. Mt Paektu, their primary site of memory, is in a sense not really yet of memory, but brought forward into the present. It will be another set of questions entirely if the framework of Korean politics, culture and memory as it currently is transforms anew. For the moment Kim Jong Suk, the new goddess and the landscape of Mt Paektu serve as a landscape of technology, self-transformation, violence, myth and power, one for our time and for all times. The Korean peninsula and North Korea's ideology and commemorative practices are still social-cultural terrains on the move. They are constantly reconfiguring themselves, as much as they seek to maintain authority and connection with the past. These Korean transformative and mythic histories are in active dialectic with past, present and future. It will be for readers in the deep future to consider whether this dialectic and these technologies, traditions, mythologies and practices are useful and functional for all time.

# Bibliography


Alter, Joseph. 2013. "Sex, *Askesis* and the Athletic Perfection of the Soul: Physical Philosophy in the Ancient Mediterranean and South Asia". In *Religion and the Subtle Body in Asia and the West: Between Mind and Body*, edited by Geoffrey Samuel and Jay Johnston, 33–47. New York: Routledge.

Anderson, Benedict. 1983. *Imagined Communities: Reflections on the Origins and Spread of Nationalism*. London: Verso.

Anonymous. 1991. *Biography of Kim Jong-suk*. Pyongyang: Foreign Languages Publishing House.

Anonymous. 2005.[46] *Biography of Kim Jong-suk*. Pyongyang: Foreign Languages Publishing House.

Arendt, Hannah. 1970. *On Violence*. Orlando, FL: Harcourt.

Árnason, Jón. 1972. *Icelandic Folktales and Legends*. Berkeley, CA: University of California Press.

Bailey, Peter. 1978. *Leisure and Class in Victorian England: Rational Recreation and the Contest for Control, 1830–1885*. London: Routledge.

Bainbridge, Simon. 2013. "Writing from the 'Perilous Edge': Romanticism and the Invention of Rock Climbing". *Romanticism* 19, no. 3: 246–60.

Baker, Don. 2007. "Internal Alchemy in the Dahn World School". In *Religions of Korea in Practice*, edited by Robert E. Buswell Jr, 508–13. Princeton, NJ: Princeton University Press.

Barth, J. Robert. 2003. *Romanticism and Transcendence: Wordsworth, Coleridge and the Religious Imagination*. Columbus, MI: University of Missouri Press.

Barthes, Roland. 1972. *Mythologies*. London: J. Cape.

Bauman, Zygmunt. 2006. *Liquid Fear*. Cambridge: Polity Press.

Bennett, Jane. 2010. *Vibrant Matter: A Political Ecology of Things*. Durham, NC: Duke University Press.

Bergin, Sean. 2009. *The Khmer Rouge and the Cambodian Genocide*. New York: Rosen Publishing.

Berthelier, Benoit. 2013. "Symbolic Truth: Epic Legends and the Making of the Baekdusan Generals". *Sino-NK*, 17 May 2013. https://sinonk.com/2013/05/17/symbolic-truth-epic-legends-and-the-making-of-the-baektusan-generals/.


---

[46] The Korean translation of the current version of the 2005 *Biography* is *Nyŏjanggun* 녀장군 (2007) which is also anonymous, but published by the Social Sciences Publishing House in Pyongyang.

Berthelier, Benoit. 2014. "Paektu Mountain and Revolutionary Mystique in North Korea since 1945". Paper presented at the Royal Geographical Society Annual Conference, London, August 2014.

Birmingham, David. 1988. *Kwame Nkrumah: The Father of African Nationalism*. Columbus, OH: Ohio University Press.

Broughton, Jeffrey. 1999. *The Bodhidharma Anthology: The Earliest Records of Zen*. Berkeley, CA: University of California Press.

Byman, Daniel, and Jennifer Lind. 2010. "Pyongyang's Survival Strategy: Tools of Authoritarian Control in North Korea". *International Security* 35, no. 1: 44–74.

Campany, Robert. 2002. *To Live as Long as Heaven and Earth: A Translation and Study of Ge Hong's Traditions of Divine Transcendents*. Berkeley, CA: University of California Press.

Campbell, Charles. 1892. "A Journey Through North Korea to the Chang-pai Shan". *Proceedings of the Royal Geographical Society and the Monthly Record of Geography* 14, no. 3: 141–61.

Caprio, Mark. 2014. *Japanese Assimilation Policies in Colonial Korea, 1910–1945*. Seattle, WA: University of Washington Press.

Castree, Noel. 2001. *Social Nature*. Malden, MA: Blackwell Publishing.

Cavendish, Alfred Edward John, and Henry Edward Goold-Adams. 1884. *Korea and the Sacred White Mountain, Being a Brief Account of a Journey in Korea in 1891, Together with an Account of an Ascent of the White Mountain*. London: George Philip & Son.

Chakravati, Sudeep. 2009. *Red Sun: Travels in Naxalite Country*. New Delhi: Penguin India.

Chang, Ju-Ho. 2002. "Korea: The Various Roles of Sport for All in Society". In *Worldwide Experiences and Trends in Sport for All*, edited by Lamartine DaCosta and Ana Miragaya, 133–74. Oxford: Meyer & Meyer Sport.

Chesneaux, Jean. 1972. "Secret Societies in China's Historical Evolution". In *Popular Movements and Secret Societies in China, 1840–1950*, edited by Jean Chesneaux, 1–28. Stanford, CA: Stanford University Press.

Chesnokova, Nataliya. 2014. "The Concept of Phungsu Chiri Seol 風水地理說 in Yi Chunghwan's 'T'aengniji'". Paper presented at the 12th Biennial Conference of Asian Studies in Israel, University of Haifa, Israel, May 2014.

Chesnokova, Nataliya. 2018. "Spatial Views and Self-Consciousness of Culture in Korea in the 18th Century. Based on the 'T'aengniji' (1751) by Yi Chung-Hwan (1690–1756?)". Doctoral dissertation, Institute for Oriental and Classical Studies, Russian State University for the Humanities, Moscow.

Chi, Hŭng-kil 지흥길. 2004. *Paektusan chonsŏljip 4: Singihan paljaguk* 백두산 전설집 4: 신기한 발자국 (Anthology of Mount Paektu Legends Volume 4: Mysterious Footprints). Pyongyang: Munhak Yesuk chulp'ansa 문학예술출판사.

Cho, Eun-so. 2013. "From Ascetic to Activist: Jiyul Sunim's Korean Buddhist Eco-Movement". In *Nature, Environment and Culture in East Asia: The Challenge of Climate Change*, edited by Carmen Meinert, 259–80. Leiden: Brill.

Cho, Hyun-soul. 2010. "The Significance of Perceptions of Baekdusan in Baekdurelated Myths". *The Review of Korean Studies* 13, no. 4: 33–52.

Cho, Pŏp-chong 조법종. 2010. "Paektusan kwa Changpaeksan, kŭrigo Manju" 백두산과 장백산, 그리고 만주 (Mount Paektu and Mount Changpaek, and Manchuria). In *Paektusan: hyŏnje wa mirae rŭl marhanda* 백두산: 현재와 미래를 말한다 (Mount Paektu: Speaking the Present and the Future), edited by Hangukhakchunganyŏnguwŏn, 35–64. Kyŏnggi-do Sŏnnam-si: Chŏnjŏggil.

Ch'oe, Chin'gu 최진구. 2013. "Silla Oak kwa Pulgyŏ ŭi *sansin sinang* yŏn'gu" 신라 五岳과 불교의 산신신앙 연구 (The Study on Five Mountains and Buddhist Beliefs in Mountain Spirits). *Silla munhwa* 新羅文化 (The Journal of the Center of Research for Silla Culture) 42: 243–68.

Ch'oe, Sŏng-jin 최성진. 2006. *Paektu kwangmyŏngsŏng chonsŏl jip 5: Hanŭlman anda* 백두광명성전설집 5: 하늘만이 안다 (Anthology of Paektu Bright Light Legends Volume 5: Only the Heaven Knows). Pyongyang: Munhak Yesuk Chulp'ansa 문학예술출판사.

Ch'oe, Unsik 최운식. 2004. "Chunnyŏng *sansindang* tangsinhwa 'Tajagu Halmŏni' wa Chunnyŏng *sansinje*" 죽령 산신당 당신화 「다자구 할머니」와 죽령 산신제 (Chunnyŏng *sansin* Mythology: Tajagu Grandmother Goddess and Chunnyŏng *sansinje*). *Han'guk minsokhak* 韓國民俗學 (Journal of Korean Folklore) 39 (2004): 381–410.

Chong, Kelly. 2008. *Deliverance and Submission: Evangelical Women and the Negotiation of Patriarchy in South Korea*. Cambridge, MA: Harvard University Asia Center.

Chŏng, Kyŏnghŭi. 2015. "Hyŏndae Tan'gun undong ŭi saeroun chŏn'gae wa Tanhak" 현대 '단군운동' 의 새로운 전개와 '丹學' (The New Development of Tan'gun Movement and Tanhak in Contemporary Korea). *Sŏndo munhwa* (Journal of Korean *Sŏndo* Culture), 2015: 143–94.

Chung, Byung-ho. 2008. "Between Defector and Migrant: Identities and Strategies of North Koreans in South Korea". *Korean Studies* 32: 1–27.

Clayton, Thomas. 1998. "Building the New Cambodia: Educational Destruction and Construction Under the Khmer Rouge, 1975–1979". *History of Education Quarterly* 38, no. 1: 1–16.

Clippinger, Morgan. 1981. "Kim Chŏng-il in the North Korean Mass Media: A Study of Semi-Esoteric Communication". *Asian Survey* 21, no. 3: 289–309.

Cosgrove, Denis. 1984. *Social Formation and Symbolic Landscape*. Madison, WI: University of Wisconsin Press.

Cosgrove, Denis. 2004. "Landscape and Landschaft". Lecture given at the "Spatial Turn in History" Symposium, German Historical Institute, February 2004.

Cosgrove, Denis. 2008. *High Places, Cultural Geographies of Mountains and Ice*. London: I.B. Tauris.

Cressey, George. 1963. *Asia's Lands and Peoples: A Geography of One-Third of the Earth and Two-Thirds of Its People*. New York: McGraw-Hill.

Cumings, Bruce. 1981. *Origins of the Korean War*, vol. 1: *Liberation and the Emergence of Separate Regimes*. Princeton, NJ: Princeton University Press.

Cumings, Bruce. 2005. *Korea's Place in the Sun*. New York: W.W. Norton.

David-Fox, Michael. 1997. *Revolution of the Mind: Higher Learning Among the Bolsheviks, 1918–1928*. Ithaca, NY: Cornell University Press.

Dax, Frank. 2015. "Recreational Hiking in South Korea: Transforming the Body, Transforming the Land". *Korea Journal* 55, no. 3: 80–102.

de Ceuster, Koen. 2011. "To Be an Artist in North Korea: Talent and Then Some More". In *Exploring North Korean Arts*, edited by Rudiger Frank, 51–71. Vienna: MAK Verlag.

de Ceuster, Koen. 2013. "South Korea's Encounter with North Korean Art: Between Barbershop Painting and True Art". In *De-Bordering Korea: Tangible and Intangible Legacies of the Sunshine Policy*, edited by Valérie Gelézeau, Koen de Ceuster and Alain Delissen, 155–71. London: Routledge.

de Ceuster, Koen. 2015. "Lost Without the Leader: Visual Narratives in North Korean Propaganda Art". Paper presented at the AKSE 2015 Biannual Conference, Bochum, Germany, July 2015.

Debarbieux, Bernard, and Gilles Rudaz. 2015. *The Mountain: A Political History from the Enlightenment to the Present*. Chicago: Chicago University Press.

Deleuze, Gilles, and Felix Guattari. 1984. *Anti-Oedipus: Capitalism and Schizophrenia*. London: Athlone Press.

Deleuze, Gilles, and Felix Guattari. 1987. *A Thousand Plateaus: Capitalism and Schizophrenia*. Minneapolis, MN: University of Minnesota Press.

Despeux, Catherine. 1990. *Immortelles de la Chine Ancienne. Taoïsme et Alchimie Féminine*. Puiseaux: Pardès.

Despeux, Catherine. 1997. "Le Qigong, une Expression de la Modernité Chinoise". In *En Suivant la Voie Royale. Mélanges en Homage à Léon Vandermeersch*, edited by J. Gernet and M. Kalinowski, 267–81. Paris: École Française d'Extrême-Orient.

Despeux, Catherine. 2008. "*Yangshen* 養生 Nourishing Life". In *The Encyclopedia of Taoism*, edited by Fabrizio Pregadio, 1148–50. New York: Routledge.

Despeux, Catherine, and Livia Kohn. 2003. *Women in Daoism*. Dunedin: Three Pines Press.

Dixon-Kennedy, Mike. 2005. *A Companion to Arthurian and Celtic Myths and Legends*. Cheltenham: History Press.

Dorrestijn, Steven. 2012. "The Design of Our Own Lives: Technical Mediation and Subjectivation After Foucault". PhD thesis, University of Twente.

Doty, William. 2000. *Mythography: The Study of Myths and Rituals*. Tuscaloosa, AL: University of Alabama Press.

Duus, Peter. 1998. *The Abacus and the Sword: The Japanese Penetration of Korea, 1895–1910*. Berkeley, CA: University of California Press.

Eliade, Mircea. 1969. *Yoga, Immortality and Freedom*. Princeton, NJ: Princeton University Press.

Elmes, Michael, and Bob Frame. 2008. "Into Hot Air: A Critical Perspective on Everest". *Human Relations* 61, no. 2: 213–41.

Em, Henry. 2013. *The Great Enterprise: Sovereignty and Historiography in Modern Korea*. Durham, NC: Duke University Press.

Fedman, David. 2015. "The Saw and the Seed: Japanese Forestry in Colonial Korea 1895–1945". Doctoral dissertation, Stanford University.

Flood, Gavin. 2004. *The Ascetic Self: Subjectivity, Memory and Tradition*. Cambridge: Cambridge University Press.

Foucault, Michel. 1977. *Discipline and Punish: The Birth of the Prison*. New York: Random House.

Foucault, Michel. 1994. "Les Techniques de Soi". In *Dits et Écrits 1954–1988. IV: 1980–1988*, 783–813. Paris: Gallimard.

Foucault, Michel. 2001. *L'Hermeneutique du sujet: Cours au Collège de France (1981–1982)*. Paris: Gallimard.

Foucault, Michel, Luther Martin, Huck Gutman and Patrick Hutton, eds. 1988. *Technologies of the Self: A Seminar with Michel Foucault*. Amherst, MA: University of Massachusetts Press.

Gabroussenko, Tatiana. 2010. *Soldiers on the Cultural Front: Developments in the Early History of North Korean Literature and Literary Policy*. Honolulu, HI: University of Hawai'i Press.

Gandy, Mathew. 2014. *The Fabric of Space*. Cambridge, MA: MIT Press.

Geertz, Clifford. 1980. *Negara: The Theatre State in Nineteenth-Century Bali*. Princeton, NJ: Princeton University Press.

Gelézeau, Valerie, Koen de Ceuster and Alain Delissen, eds. 2013. *(De)Bordering Korea: Tangible and Intangible Legacies of the Sunshine Policy*. London: Routledge.

Golomstock, Igor. 1990. *Totalitarian Art*. New York: Overlook Press.

Gorriti, Gustavo. 2000. *The Shining Path: A History of the Millenarian War in Peru*. Chapel Hill, NC: University of North Carolina Press.

Gragert, Edwin. 1994. *Landownership Under Japanese Rule: Korea's Colonial Experience 1910–1935*. Honolulu: University of Hawai'i Press.

Graves, Robert. 1955. *The Greek Myths*. London: Penguin.

Grundy-Warr, Carl, and Elaine Wong Siew Yin. 2002. "Geographies of Displacement: The Karenni and Shan Across the Myanmar–Thailand Border". *Singapore Journal of Tropical Geography* 23, no. 1: 93–122.

Han, Ju Hui Judy. 2010. "Neither Friends Nor Foes: Thoughts on Ethnographic Distance". *Geoforum* 41, no. 1: 11–14.

Han, Ju Hui Judy. 2013. "Beyond Safe Haven: A Critique of Christian Custody of North Korean Migrants in China". *Critical Asian Studies* 45, no. 4: 533–60.

Han, Ju Hui Judy, and Jennifer Jihye Chun. 2014. "Introduction: Gender and Politics in Contemporary Korea". *Journal of Korean Studies* 19, no. 2: 245–55.

Harraway, Donna. 1991. *Simians, Cyborgs and Women: The Reinvention of Nature*. New York: Routledge.

Haruki, Wada. 1992. *Kin Nissei To Manshu Konichi Senso* (Kim Il Sung and the Manchurian Anti-Japanese War). Tokyo: Heibonsha.

Havrelock, Richard, 2011. *River Jordan: The Mythology of a Dividing Line*. Chicago: University of Chicago Press.

Hobsbawm, Eric, and Terence Ranger. 1983. *The Invention of Tradition*. Cambridge: Cambridge University Press.

Ilyon. 1972. *Samguk Yusa: Legends and History of the Three Kingdoms of Ancient Korea*. Seoul: Yonsei University Press.

Im, Chaehae 임재해, and Chongsŏng Pak 박종성. 2005. "*Sansin* sŏrhwa ŭi chŏnsŭng yangsang kwa *sansin* sungbae ŭi munhwa" 산신설화의 전승양상과 산신숭배의 문화

(The Transmission of Mountain Gods Folktales and the Culture of Mountain Gods Worship). *Pikyo minsokhak* 比較民俗學 (Asian Comparative Folklore) 29: 379–423.

James, Henry. 1888. *The Long White Mountain, Or, A Journey in Manchuria: With Some Account of the History, People, Administration and Religion of that Country.* London: Longman, Green & Co.

Jo, Yoong-hee, 2009. "Perceptions of Choson Korea in Western Travelogues". *SOAS-AKS Working Papers in Korean Studies*, 8. London: SOAS, University of London.

Johnston, Jay. 2013. "Introduction to Part Four". In *Religion and the Subtle Body in Asia and the West: Between Mind and Body*, edited by Geoffrey Samuel and Jay Johnston, 187–91. New York: Routledge.

Joinau, Benjamin. 2014. "'The Arrow and the Sun': A Topo-Myth Analysis of Pyongyang". *Sungkyun Journal of East Asian Studies* 14, no. 1: 65–92.

Jongheon, Jin. 2005. "The Transforming Sacredness of Mount Chirisan from a Utopian Shelter into a Modern National Park: Focused on the Escapist Lives of 'Mountain Men'". *Journal of the Korean Geographical Society* 40, no. 2: 172–86.

Kang, Sŏkhwa 강석화. 2011. "Chosŏn hugi Paektusan e taehan insik ŭi pyŏnhwa" 조선 후기 백두산에 대한 인식의 변화 (Changes in the Perception of Paektu Mountain in Late Chosŏn). *Chosŏn sidae sa hakpo* (The Journal of Chosŏn Dynasty History) 30: 195–224.

Kang, Sŏngbok 강성복. 2011. "Kongju Tonghaeri *sanhyangkye* ŭi sŏngnip kwa *sansinje* ŭi pyŏnhwa" 공주 동해리 산향계의 성립과 산신제의 변화 (Establishment of *Sanhyangkye* in Kongju Tonghaeri and the Changes in *Sansinje*). *Han'guk minsokhak* 韓國民俗學 (Journal of Korean Folklore) 54: 7–36.

Kang, Tong-gu 강동구. 2000. "Saeroun sinhwa mandŭlgi – *chaeya sahak* e taehan tto tarŭn ihae" 새로운 신화 믄들기 – 재야사학에 대한 또 드른 이해 (Making a New Myth: Another View on the *Chaya Sahak*). *Chŏngsin munhwa yŏn'gu* 정신문화연구 (Korean Studies Quarterly) 23, no. 1: 3–16.

KCNA. 2013. "DPRK Hero Title Awarded to Traffic Controller". *KCNA*, 5 May 2013. Accessed 24 July 2015.

KCNA. 2017a. "Wreaths Laid at Bust of Kim Jong Suk". *KCNA*, 24 December 2017. http://www.kcna.co.jp/item/2017/201712/news22/2017124-14ee.html.[47]

---

[47] Korean Central News Agency, North Korea's state news agency has several websites. In 2010 KCNA established a .kp address registered in North Korea, but this did not supersede the original http://www.kcna.co.jp address as this Japanese registered version has a searchable database going back some 18 years whereas the North Korea site only has the current years stories. Recently the http://www.kcna.co.jp site has been unavailable as it has been geo-blocked so that only browsers and computers accessing it from a Japanese Internet connection can access it (NorthKoreaTech has a report on this at https://www.northkoreatech. org/2015/08/09/kcna-japan-site-isnt-down-its-geo-blocked/. This was extremely frustrating to all that use it and enabled the commodification of the database through paywalled access sites such as kcnawatch. The fact that it should only be available from Japanese computers, however, is not a barrier to using it outside of Japan, so instead of paying to access these links, use a VPN like Tor, or install the Hola extension on Google Chrome and set it to spoof your Internet connection so that it looks as if you are browsing from Japan. http://www.kcna. co.jp will then be free and accessible to you anywhere in the world. Download Hola from http://www.hola.org, download Tor from http://www.torproject.org.

KCNA. 2017b. "Kim Jong Suk's Birth Anniversary Marked in Hoeryong". *KCNA*, 24 December 2017. http://www.kcna.co.jp/item/2017/201712/ news22/2017122-12ee.html.

KCNA. 2017c. "Kim Jong Suk, Outstanding Woman Revolutionary". *KCNA*, 23 December 2017. http://www.kcna.co.jp/item/2017/201712/news23/2017123-15ee.html.

KCNA. 2017d. "Coins to be Minted in DPRK to Mark Kim Jong Suk's 100th Birthday". *KCNA*, 22 December 2017. http://www.kcna.co.jp/item/2017/201712/ news22/2017122-20ee.html.

KCNA. 2017e. "Mementoes Associated with Immortal Feats of Kim Jong Suk". *KCNA*, 22 December 2017. http://www.kcna.co.jp/item/2017/201712/ news22/2017122-11ee.html.

Kendall, Laurel. 1987. *Shamans, Housewives, and Other Restless Spirits*. Honolulu: University of Hawai'i Press.

Kendall, Laurel. 2009. "The Global Reach of Gods and the Travels of Korean Shamans". In *Transnational Transcendence: Essays on Religion and Globalization*, edited by Thomas J. Csordas, 305–25. Berkeley, CA: University of California Press.

Keum, Jang-tae. 1994. "Mountains: Home of Korean Thought". *Koreana*, 8, no. 4: 10–17.

Kim Jong Il, 2012. *Anecdotes of Kim Jong Il's Life*. Pyongyang: Foreign Languages Publishing House.

Kim Il Sung, 1964. *Works*, vol. 18. Pyongyang: Foreign Languages Publishing House.

Kim, Chŏngha 김정하. 2007. "Injegun *sansinje* ŭi sigi mit kusŏng wŏlli koch'al" 인제 군 산신제(山神祭)의 시기 및 구성 원리 고찰 (A Study on the Structure of *Sansinje* in Inje County). *Kangwŏn minsokhak* 강원민속학 (The Kangwŏn Province Folklore) 21: 145–66.

Kim, Daeyeol, 2000. "Symbolisme de la force vitale en Chine ancienne. Modèles et significations dans l'alchimie taoïste opératoire: études des pratiques alchimiques du Baopuzi neipian 抱朴子内篇 (4e siècle après J.-C. en Chine)". Doctoral thesis, Université de Paris-Sorbonne (Paris 4).

Kim, Duk-muk. 2004. "Bukhansan Keeps Alive Shaman Traditions". *Koreana* 18, no. 1: 10–11.

Kim, Kang-san 김강산. 2006. "T'aebaek sansin i toen Tanjong" 태백산신이 된 단종 (King Tanjong Becoming a God of T'aebak Mountain). *Kangwŏn minsokhak* 강원 민속학 (The Kangwŏn Province Folklore) 20: 361–85.

Kim, Nayeon. 2012. "Indoctrinating Female Virtue: The Social Use of Chosŏn Woodblock Prints". Paper presented at the Eighth Worldwide Consortium of Korean Studies Centers Workshop, July 2012, Seoul.

Kim, Sŏn-p'ung 김선풍. 2003. "Tan'gun sinhwa wa T'aebaeksan, Mokmyŏksan, Samgaksan sinhwa ŭi taebi punsŏk" 단군신화와 태백산·목멱산·삼각산신화의 대 비분석 (A Comparative Study on Tan'gun Legend and the Legends of T'aebaek, Mokmyŏk and Samgak Mountains). *Kangwŏn minsokhak* 강원민속학 (The Kangwŏn Province Folklore) 17: 73–102.

Kim, Suzy. 2013. *Everyday Life in the North Korea Revolution: 1945–1950*. Ithaca, NY: Cornell University Press.

Kim, Suzy. 2014. "Mothers and Maidens: Gendered Formation of Revolutionary Heroes in North Korea". *Journal of Korean Studies* 19, no. 2: 257–89.

Kim, Yŏng-ja 김영자. 2005. "*Sansindo* e p'yohyŏntoen *sansin* ŭi yuhyŏng" 산신도 (山神圖)에 표현된 산신(山神)의 유형 (Various Types of Mountain God Depicted in Paintings). *Han'guk minsokhak* 韓國民俗學 (Journal of Korean Folklore) 41: 187–223.

Kirkland, Russell. 1991. "The Making of an Immortal: The Exaltation of Ho Chih-chang". *Numen* 38, no. 2: 214–30.

Kirkland, Russell. 2008. "Transcendence and Immortality". In *The Encyclopedia of Taoism*, edited by Fabrizio Pregadio, 91–3. New York: Routledge.

Kwon, Heonik. 2013. "North Korea's New Legacy Politics". *E-International Relations*, 16 May 2013. https://www.e-ir.info/2013/05/16/north-koreas-new-legacy-politics/.

Kwon, Heonik, and Byung-ho Chung. 2012. *North Korea: Beyond Charismatic Politics*. Lanham, MD: Rowman & Littlefield.

Kwŏn, T'ae-hyo 권태효. 1998. "Hoguk *yŏsansin* sŏrhwa ŭi sangbantoen sin'gyŏk insik yangsang yŏn'gu" 호국여산신설화의 상반된 신격 인식 양상 연구 (A Study on a Contradictory Character of the Legends Depicting Goddesses Protecting the State). *Han'guk minsokhak* 韓國民俗學 (Journal of Korean Folklore) 30: 221–43.

Kyle, Gerard, Alan Graefe, Robert Manning and James Bacon. 2003. "An Examination of the Relationship Between Leisure Activity and Place Attachment among Hikers along the Appalachian Trail". *Journal of Leisure Research* 35, no. 3: 249–73.

Lankov, Andrei. 2007. *North of the DMZ: Essays on Daily Life in North Korea*. Jefferson, NC: Macfarland.

Lee, Chong-Sik. 1982. "Evolution of the Korean Workers' Party and the Rise of Kim Chŏng-il". *Asian Survey* 22, no. 5: 434–48.

Lee, Ki-baik. 1984. *A New History of Korea*. Cambridge, MA: Harvard University Press.

Lee, Peter, and Wm. Theodore de Bary, eds. 1997. *Sources of Korean Tradition*, vol. 1: *From Early Times Through the Sixteenth Century*. New York: Columbia University Press.

Lee, Su-hoon. 1999. "Environmental Movements in South Korea". In *Asian Environmental Movements*, edited by Yok-shiu Lee and A. Armonk So, 90–119. New York: M. E. Sharpe.

Lefebvre, Henri. 1991. *The Production of Space*. Malden, MA: Blackwell Publishing.

Lett, Denise. 1998. *In Pursuit of Status: The Making of South Korea's "New" Urban Middle Class*. Cambridge, MA: Harvard University Asia Center.

Lim, Jae-Cheon. 2015. *Leader Symbols and Personality Cult in North Korea*. London: Routledge.

Lobetti, Tullio. 2014. *Ascetic Practices in Japanese Religion*. London: Routledge.

Lorimer, Jamie. 2007. "Non-human Charisma". *Environment and Planning D: Society and Space* 25, no. 5: 911–32.

Maguire, Jack. 2001. *Essential Buddhism*. New York: Pocket Books.

Marston, Sallie. 2000. "The Social Construction of Scale". *Progress in Human Geography* 24, no. 2: 219–41.

Mason, David. 1999. *Spirit of the Mountains*. Seoul: Hollym.

Miller, Carl. 1963. "Korean Mountains". *Korea Journal* 3, no. 9: 26–8.

Miura, Kunio. 2008a. "*Shenren* 神人 Divine Man; Spirit Man". In *The Encyclopedia of Taoism*, edited by Fabrizio Pregadio, 885–6. New York: Routledge.

Miura, Kunio, 2008b. "*Xianren* 仙人 Immortal; Transcendent". In *The Encyclopedia of Taoism*, edited by Fabrizio Pregadio, 1092–4. New York: Routledge.

Morin, Karen, Robyn Longhurst and Lynda Johnston. 2010. "(Troubling) Spaces of Mountains and Men: New Zealand's Mount Cook and Hermitage Lodge". *Social and Cultural Geography* 2, no. 2: 117–39.

Munakata, Kiyohiko. 1991. *Sacred Mountains in Chinese Art: An Exhibition Organized by the Krannert Art Museum at the University of Illinois and curated by Kiyohiko Munakata: Krannert Art Museum, November 9–December 16, 1990, The Metropolitan Museum of Art, January 25–March 31, 1991*. Urbana, IL: University of Illinois Press.

Myers, Brian Reynolds, 2011. *The Cleanest Race: How North Koreans See Themselves and Why it Matters*. New York: Melville House.

Na, Kwŏnsu 나권수. 2012. "Han'guk sinjonggyŏ ŭi *sŏndo* sasang yŏn'gu" 한국 신종교의 선도사상 연구 (A Study on *Sŏndo* Thought in Korean New Religions). *Sŏndo munhwa* 선도문화 (Journal of Korean *Sŏndo* Culture) 12: 409–43.

Naess, Arne, 2013. *The Ecology of Wisdom: Writings by Arne Naess*. Berkeley, CA: Counterpoint.

Nelson, John. 2015. *A Year in the Life of a Shinto Shrine*. Seattle, WA: University of Washington Press.

North Korean Leadership Watch. 2017. "Kim Jong Suk's 100th Birth Anniversary Marked". *North Korean Leadership Watch*, 25 December 2017. http://www.nkleadershipwatch. org/2017/12/25/kim-jong-suks-100th-birth-anniversary-marked/.

Oh, Kong Dan. 1990. "North Korea in 1989: Touched by Winds of Change?" *Asian Survey* 30, no. 1: 74–80.

Ortner, Sherry. 1999. *Life and Death on Mount Everest: Sherpas and Himalayan Mountaineering*. Princeton, NJ: Princeton University Press.

Pai, Hyung-il. 2000. *Constructing "Korean" Origins: A Critical Review of Archaeology, Historiography, and Racial Myth in Korean State-Formation Theories*. Cambridge, MA: Harvard University Press.

Paik, Nak-chung. 2011. *The Division System in Crisis*. Berkeley, CA: University of California Press.

Pak, Ch'ansŭng. 2013. "Paektusanŭi 'minjok yŏngsan' ŭroŭi p'yŏsanghwa" 백두산의 '민족 영산' 으로의 표상화 (Depicting Mount Paektu as a "National Sacred Mountain). *Tongasia munhwa yŏngu* (Journal of East Asian Cultures) 55: 9–36.

Pak, Chong-ik 박종익. 2009. "Musŏngsan *sansinje* ŭi hyŏngsŏng kwa pyŏnch'ŏn" 무성산 산신제의 형성과 변천 (The Establishment and Transformation of Musŏng Mountain *Sansinje*). *Han'guk minsokhak* 韓國民俗學 (Journal of Korean Folklore) 49: 247–74.

Palais, James. 1996. *Confucian Statecraft and Korean Institutions: Yu Hyŏngwŏn and the Late Chosŏn Dynasty*. Seattle, WA: University of Washington Press.

Palmer, David. 2007. *Qigong Fever: Body, Science, and Utopia in China*. New York: Columbia University Press.

Park, Carey 박계리. 2011. "Paektusan: mandŭrŏjin chŏnt'ong kwa p'yŏsa" 백두산: 만들어진 전통과 표상 (Paektu Mountain: The Invention of Tradition and the Symbolism). *Misulsa Hakpo* (Korean Journal of Art History) 36: 43–74.

Park, Han S. 2007. "Military-First Politics (Songun): Understanding Kim Jong-il's North Korea". *KEI Academic Paper Series* 2, no. 7: 1–9.

Park, Han S. 2012. *North Korea: The Politics of Unconventional Wisdom*. Boulder, Co: Lynne Reinner.

Park, Hyun-ok. 2005. *Two Dreams in One Bed: Empire, Social Life and the Origins of the North Korean Revolution in Manchuria*. Durham, NC: Duke University Press.

Peiker, Piret. 2016. "Estonian Nationalism through the Postcolonial Lens". *Journal of Baltic Studies* 47, no. 1: 113–32.

Poole, Janet. 2014. *When the Future Disappears: The Modernist Imagination in Late Colonial Korea*. New York: Columbia University Press.

Portal, Jane. 2005. *Art Under Control in North Korea*. London: Reaktion.

Pregadio, Fabrizio. 2008. "*Dantian* 丹田 Cinnabar field(s); Fields of the Elixir". In *The Encyclopedia of Taoism*, edited by Fabrizio Pregadio, 302–3. New York: Routledge.

Reader, Ian. 2013. *Pilgrimage in the Marketplace*. New York: Routledge.

Rodong Sinmun. 2014.[48] "Leading Party Officials Start Study Tour of Revolutionary Battle Sites on Mt Paektu". *Rodong Sinmun*, 31 July 2014. http://www.rodong.rep.kp/en/index.php?strPageID=SF01_02_0&newsID=2014-07-31-0006.

Rodong Sinmun. 2015a. "The 250 Mile Schoolchildren's March". *Rodong Sinmun*, 23 January 2015. http://www.rodong.rep.kp/en/index.php?strPageID=SF01_02_01&newsID=2015-01-23-0004.

Rodong Sinmun. 2015b. "The Schoolchildren's March reaches Kanggye". *Rodong Sinmun*, 3 February 2015. http://www.rodong.rep.kp/en/index.php?strPageID=SF01_02_01&newsID=2015-02-03-0004.

Rodong Sinmun. 2015c. "The Schoolchildren's March reaches Phophyong". *Rodong Sinmun*, 5 February 2015. http://www.rodong.rep.kp/en/index.php?strPageID=SF01_02_01&newsID=2015-02-05-0007.

Rodong Sinmun. 2016. "Kim Jong Suk Library Opens to the Public in Cuba". *Rodong Sinmun*, 2 December 2016. http://rodong.rep.kp/en/index.php?strPageID=SF01_02_01&newsID=2016-12-02-0005.

Rodong Sinmun. 2018a. "Dancing Parties of Youth and Students Held". *Rodong Sinmun*, 18 April 2018. http://rodong.rep.kp/en/index.php?strPageID=SF01_02_01&newsID=2018-04-18-0012.

Rodong Sinmun. 2018b. "Schoolchildren's Study Tour Starts". *Rodong Sinmun*,

[48] It must be acknowledged that due to North Korea's habit of wiping the database of *Rodong Sinmun* articles every year or two, the author cannot guarantee that articles from *Rodong Sinmun* will still be available at the web addresses given. The author, however, keeps a copy of each *Rodong Sinmun* article in a word document and would be happy to share any with interested readers. It is also worth acknowledging that these are the English language versions of the *Rodong Sinmun* articles, Korean language versions of course exist and the author has copies of all of these as well. Again the author would be willing to share these with interested readers.

17 March 2018. http://rodong.rep.kp/en/index.php?strPageID=SF01_02_01 &newsID=2018-03-17-0003.

Rodong Sinmun. 2018c. "Schoolchildren Visit Mangyongdae". *Rodong Sinmun*, 9 June 2018. http://rodong.rep.kp/en/index.php?strPageID=SF01_02_01 &newsID=2018-06-09-0004.

Rodong Sinmun. 2018d. "Youth and Students Make Study Tour of Revolutionary Battle Sites in Mt Paektu". *Rodong Sinmun*, 26 June 2018. http://rodong.rep.kp/en/index. php?strPageID=SF01_02_01&newsID=2018-06-26-0003.

Rodong Sinmun. 2018e. "Officials and Members of Agricultural Workers Union Tour Area of Mt Paektu". *Rodong Sinmun*, 16 August 2018. http://rodong.rep.kp/en/ index.php?strPageID=SF01_02_01&newsID=2018-08-16-0020.

Rodong Sinmun. 2018f. "Pak Pong Ju Inspects Samjiyon County and Tanchon Power Station under Construction". *Rodong Sinmun*, 11 August 2018. http://rodong.rep. kp/en/index.php?strPageID=SF01_02_01&newsID=2018-08-11-0009.

Rodong Sinmun. 2018g. "Pak Pong Ju Inspects Construction Sites in Samjiyon County". *Rodong Sinmun*, 4 April 2018. http://rodong.rep.kp/en/index.php?strPageID=SF01_ 02_01&newsID=2018-04-04-0008.

Rodong Sinmun, 2018h. "The Revolutionary Opera Played Successfully". *Rodong Sinmun*, 23 November 2018. http://rodong.rep.kp/en/index.php?strPageID=SF01_ 02_01&newsID=2018-11-23-0013.

Rodong Sinmun. 2018i. "Kim Jong Un Inspects Sinuiiju Textile Mill". *Rodong Sinmun*, 2 July 2018. http://rodong.rep.kp/en/index.php?strPageID=SF01_02_01 &newsID=2018-07-02-0002.

Rodong Sinmun. 2019. "School Youth and Children Start Study Tour of Chairman Kim Jong Il's Birthplace". *Rodong Sinmun*, 2 February 2019. http://rodong.rep.kp/en/ index.php?strPageID=SF01_02_01&newsID=2019-02-02-0008.

Rodong Sinmun. 2020a. "Schoolchildren Start March along Course of 250-mile Journey for National Liberation". *Rodong Sinmun*, 23 January 2020. http://rodong. rep.kp/en/index.php?strPageID=SF01_02_01&newsID=2020-01-23-0001.

Rodong Sinmun. 2020b. "Schoolchildren on Tour of 250-mile Journey for National Liberation Pass Hyangsan". *Rodong Sinmun*, 26 January 2020. http://rodong.rep. kp/en/index.php?strPageID=SF01_02_01&newsID=2020-01-26-0004.

Rodong Sinmun. 2020c. "Schoolchildren on Expedition of 250-mile Journey for National Liberation Arrives in Kanggye". *Rodong Sinmun*, 1 February 2020. http:// rodong.rep.kp/en/index.php?strPageID=SF01_02_01&newsID=2020-02-01-0002.

Rodong Sinmun. 2020d. "Schoolchildren's Expedition Group Arrives in Phophyong". *Rodong Sinmun*, 4 February 2020. http://rodong.rep.kp/en/index.php?strPageID= SF01_02_01&newsID=2020-02-04-0009.

Rodong Sinmun. 2020e. "UAWK Officials Start Tour of Revolutionary Battle Sites in Area of Mt Paektu". *Rodong Sinmun*, 28 January 2020. http://rodong.rep.kp/en/ index.php?strPageID=SF01_02_01&newsID=2020-01-28-0001.

Rodong Sinmun. 2020f. "Youth League Officials Start Expedition to Revolutionary Battle Sites in Area of Mt Paektu". *Rodong Sinmun*, 16 February 2020. http:// rodong.rep.kp/en/index.php?strPageID=SF01_02_01&newsID=2020-02-16-0004.

Rodong Sinmun. 2020g. "Commanding Officers of KPISF Tour Revolutionary Battle

Sites in Mt Paektu Area". *Rodong Sinmun*, 8 February 2020. http://rodong.rep.kp/en/index.php?strPageID=SF01_02_01&newsID=2020-02-08-0009.

Róna-Tas, András. 1999. "Chuvash and Historical Morphology". *Acta Orientalia Academiae Scientiarum Hungaricae* 52, no. 1: 1–15.

Rose, Deborah. 1996. *Nourishing Terrains: Australian Aboriginal Views of Landscape and Wilderness*. Canberra: Australian Heritage Commission.

Ryu, Je-Hun, and Doo-Hee Won. 2013. "The Modern Production of Multiple Meanings of the Baekdudaegan Mountain System". *Korea Journal* 53, no. 3: 103–32.

Schafer, Edward. 1980. *The Divine Woman: Dragon Ladies and Rain Maidens in T'ang Literature*. San Francisco: North Point Press.

Schattschneider, Ellen. 2003. *Immortal Wishes: Labour and Transcendence on a Japanese Sacred Mountain*. Durham, NC: Duke University Press.

Scheid, Volker. 2002. *Chinese Medicine in Contemporary China: Plurality and Synthesis*. Durham, NC: Duke University Press.

Schipper, Kristofer. 1993. *The Taoist Body*. Berkeley, CA: University of California Press.

Schmid, Andre. 2007. "Tributary Relations and the Qing–Chosun Frontier on Mount Paektu". In *The Chinese State at the Borders*, edited by Diana Lary, 126–49. Vancouver: University of British Columbia Press.

Seiler, Sydney A. 1994. *Kim Il-sŏng 1941–1948: The Creation of a Legend, the Building of a Regime*. London: University Press of America.

Seth, Michael. 2006. *A Concise History of Korea: From the Neolithic Period Through the Nineteenth Century*. Lanham, MD: Rowman & Littlefield.

Shahar, Meir. 2008. *The Shaolin Monastery: History, Religion and the Chinese Martial Arts*. Honolulu: University of Hawai'i Press.

Shapiro, Judith. 2001. *Mao's War Against Nature: Politics and Environment in Revolutionary China*. Cambridge: Cambridge University Press.

Shepherd, Roger. 2010. "Rediscovering Korean Mountain Spirituality". *Seoul Magazine*, June: 25–6.

Shim, David. 2013. *Visual Politics and North Korea: Seeing is Believing*. London: Routledge.

Shin, Gi-wook. 2014. *Peasant Protest and Social Change in Colonial Korea*. Seattle, WA: University of Washington Press.

Shinn, Rin-Sup. 1982. "North Korea in 1981: First Year for De Facto Successor Kim Jong Il". *Asian Survey* 22, no. 1: 99–106.

Simpson, Jacqueline. 1978. "Fifty British Dragon Tales: An Analysis". *Folklore* 89, no. 1: 79–93.

Smith, Hazel. 2015. *North Korea: Markets and Military Rule*. Cambridge: Cambridge University Press.

Smith, John. 1969. "Time, Times, and the 'Right Time'; Chronos and Kairos". *The Monist* 53, no. 1: 1–13.

Smith, Pamela. 2002. *The Body of the Artisan: Art and Experience in Scientific Revolution*. Chicago: The University of Chicago Press.

Smith, Pamela. 2014. "Knowledge in Motion". In *Cultures in Motion*, edited by

D. Rodgers, B. Raman and H. Reimitz, 109–33. Princeton, NJ: Princeton University Press.

Snyder, Gary. 1980. "Foreword". In *The Divine Woman: Dragon Ladies and Rain Maidens in T'ang Literature*, by Edward Schafer, i–xvi. San Francisco: North Point Press.

Sondŏ munhwa yŏn'guwŏn 선도문화연구원 (Research Institute of *Sŏndo* Culture), ed. 2006. *Han'guk sŏndo ŭi yŏksa wa munhwa* 한국선도의 역사와 문화 (History and Culture of Korean *Sŏndo*). Ch'ŏnan: International Graduate University for Peace Press.

Song, Nianshen. 2017. "Imagined Territory: Paektusan in Late Chosŏn Maps and Writings". *Studies in the History of Gardens & Designed Landscapes* 37, no. 2: 157–73.

Song, Nianshen. 2018. *Making Borders in Modern East Asia: The Tumen River Demarcation, 1881–1919*. Cambridge: Cambridge University Press.

Song, Yong-tŏk, 2007. "The Recognition of Mountain Baekdu in the Koryo Dynasty and Early Times of the Joseon Dynasty". *History and Reality* 64: 127–59.

Sorensen, Clark W. 1988. *Over the Mountains are Mountains: Korean Peasant Households and Their Adaptations to Rapid Industrialization*. Seattle, WA: University of Washington Press.

Squire, Shelach. 1988. "Wordsworth and Lake District Tourism: Romantic Reshaping of Landscape". *The Canadian Geographer* 32, no. 3: 237–47.

Stoddard, Robert, and Alan Morinis. 1997. *Sacred Places, Sacred Spaces: The Geography of Pilgrimages*. Baton Rouge, LA: Louisiana State University.

Suh, Dae-sook. 1995. *Kim Il Sung: The North Korean Leader*. New York: Columbia University Press.

Swyngedouw, Erik. 1997. "Excluding the Other: The Production of Scale and Scaled Politics". In *Geographies of Economies*, edited by Roger Lee and Jane Wills, 167–76. London: Arnold.

Swyngedouw, Erik. 2015. *Liquid Power*. Cambridge, MA: MIT Press.

Talbot, J., S. Self and C. Wilson. 1994. "Dilute Gravity Current and Rain-Flushed Ash Deposits in the 1.8 ka Hatepe Plinian Deposit, Taupo, New Zealand". *Bulletin of Volcanology* 56, no. 6: 538–51.

Toby, Ronald. 1974. "Education in Korea Under the Japanese: Attitudes and Manifestations". *Occasional Papers on Korea* (Center for Korean Research in the Weatherhead East Asian Studies Institute) 1: 55–64.

Tuan, Yi-Fu. 1998. *Escapism*. Baltimore, MD: Johns Hopkins University Press.

Turner, Victor. 1969. *The Ritual Process: Structure and Anti-Structure*. Chicago: Aldine.

Valantasis, Richard. 1995. "A Theory of the Social Function of Asceticism". In *Asceticism*, edited by Vincent L. Wimbush and Richard Valantasis, 544–52. Oxford: Oxford University Press.

Valenius, Johanna. 2004. *Undressing the Maid: Gender, Sexuality, and the Body in the Construction of the Finnish Nation*. Vol. 85. Finnish Literature Society.

Van der Veer, Peter. 2007. "Global Breathing: Religious Utopias in India and China". *Anthropological Theory* 7, no. 3: 315–29.

Vasilyev, L. S. 1970. *Kulti, religii i tradizii v Kitae* Культы, религии и традиции в Китае (Cults, Religions and Traditions in China). Moscow: Nauka Наука.

Verellen, Franciscus. 1995. "The Beyond Within: Grotto-Heavens (dongtian) in Taoist Ritual". *Cahiers d'Extrême-Asie* 8: 265–90.

Von Rad, Gerhard. 1991. *Holy War in Ancient Israel*. Grand Rapids, MI: Eerdmans.

Weber, Max. 1967. *The Theory of Economic and Social Organisation*. New York: Free Press.

Welz, Martin. 2013. *Integrating Africa: Decolonization's Legacy, Sovereignty and the African Union*. London: Routledge.

Whatmore, Sarah. 2005. *Hybrid Geographies: Natures, Cultures, Spaces*. London: Sage.

Williams, John. 1860. *Annales Cambriae*. London: Longman, Green & Co.

Winichakul, Thongchai. 1994. *Siam Mapped: A History of the Geo-Body of a Nation*. Honolulu: University of Hawai'i Press.

Winstanley-Chesters, Robert. 2014. *Environment, Politics and Ideology in North Korea: Landscape as Political Project*. Lanham, MD: Lexington Press.

Winstanley-Chesters, Robert. 2015. "'Patriotism Begins with a Love of Courtyard': Rescaling Charismatic Landscapes in North Korea". *Tiempo Devorado (Consumed Time)* 2, no. 2: 116–38.

Winstanley-Chesters, Robert. 2016. "Charisma in a Watery Frame: North Korean Narrative Topographies and the Tumen River". *Asian Perspective* 40, no. 3: 393–414.

Winstanley-Chesters, Robert, and Victoria Ten. 2016. "New Goddesses at Mt Paektu: Two Contemporary Korean Myths". *S/N Korean Humanities* 2, no. 1: 151–79.

Women of Korea. 1986. "Daughter of Korea". *Women of Korea* 1986, no. 4.

Women of Korea. 1987a. "Pak Su Hwan: Woman Anti-Japanese Revolutionary Fighter". *Women of Korea* 1987, no 4.

Women of Korea. 1987b. "The Brilliant Last: Anti-Japanese Revolutionary Fighter Li Gye Sun". *Women of Korea* 1987, no. 1.

Women of Korea. 1987c. "Woman Revolutionary Fighter Pak Rok Gum". *Women of Korea* 1987, no. 1.

Women of Korea. 1988. "Chon Hui, Anti-Japanese Revolutionary Martyr". *Women of Korea* 1988, no. 4.

Women of Korea. 1990a. "A Guerrilla Amazon: On Kim Hwak Sil, an Anti-Japanese Revolutionary Fighter". *Women of Korea* 1990, no. 1.

Women of Korea. 1990b. "Eternity". *Women of Korea* 1990, no. 2.

Women of Korea. 1991. "Liberty, Then Life Counts". *Women of Korea* 1991, no. 3.

Xu, Jiandong, Bo Pan, Tanzhuo Liu, Irka Hajdas, Bo Zhao, Hongmei Yu, Ruoxin Liu and Ping Zhao. 2013. "Climatic Impact of the Millennium Eruption of Changbaishan Volcano in China: New Insights from High-Precision Radiocarbon Wiggle-Match Dating". *Geophysical Research Letters* 40, no. 1: 54–9.

Xue Juzheng. 1976. *Jiu Wi Dai Shi* (Old History of the Five Dynasties). Beijing: Zhonghua Shu Ju.

Yanpeng, Janpeng, Paul Waley and Sara Gonzalez. 2016. "Shifting Land-Based Coalitions in Shanghai's Second Hub". *Cities* 52: 30–8.

Yecies, Brian, and Ae-gyung Shim. 2011. *Korea's Occupied Cinemas 1893–1948: The Untold History of the Film Industry*. London: Routledge.

Yi Chung-hwan. 1998. *Taengniji: The Korean Classic for Choosing Settlements*. Translated by Inshil Choe Yoon. Sydney: Wild Peony.

Yi Chung-hwan. 2019. *A Place to Live: A New Translation of Yi Chung-hwan's T'aengniji, the Korean Classic for Choosing Settlements*. Translated by Inshil Choe Yoon. Honolulu: University of Hawai'i Press.

Yi, Kyŏng-yŏp 이경엽. 2000. "Sunch'ŏn ŭi Sŏnghwang sinang, *sansin sinang* kwa yŏksa chŏk inmul ŭi singyŏkhwa" 순천의 성황신앙、산신신앙과 역사적 인물의 신격화 (The Cult of Sŏnghwang, *Sansin Sinang* and the Divinisation of Historical Figures). *Namdo minsok yŏn'gu* 남도민속연구 (Namdo Folklore Research) 6: 165–93.

Yi, Myŏngbok 이명복. 1988. *Tanhak haksŭppŏp* 단학 학습법 (The Study of Tanhak). Seoul: Taeyang 대양.

Yi, Sŏhaeng. 2010. "Paektusan ŭi hyŏnjaejŏk ŭiŭi" 백두산의 현대적 의의 (Contemporary Significance of Mount Paektu). In *Paektusan: hyŏnjae wa mirae rŭl marhanda* 백두산: 현재와 미래를 말한다 (Mount Paektu: Speaking the Present and the Future), edited by Hangukhakchunganyŏnguwŏn, 108–27. Kyŏnggi-do Sŏnnam-si: Chŏnjŏggil.

Yi, Sŭngho 이승호. 2015. *Han'guk sŏndo wa hyŏndae Tanhak* 한국 선도와 현대 단학 (Korean *Sŏndo* and Contemporary *Tanhak*). Seoul: Kukhak charyowŏn 국학 자료원.

Yi, Tôngmu. 1966. Ch'ŏngjanggwan chŏnsŏ 菁莊館全書. Seoul: Sŏul Taehakkyo Kochŏn Kanhaenghoe.

Yi, Yohan 이요한. 1987. "Han'gukin ŭi san sinang e taehan ihae" 한국인의 산 신앙에 대한 이해 (Understanding Korean Mountain Cults). *Kidokkyo Sasang* 기독교사상 (Korean Christian Thought) 343: 146–55.

Yi, Yŏnghun. 2006. "Woe tasi haebang chonhusa inka" 왜 다시 해방 전후사인가 (Why Again Pre- and Post-Liberation History). In *Haebang Chŏnhusa Cheinsiki* 해방 전후사의 재인식 (New Perception of Pre- and Post-Liberation History), edited by Chihyang Pak, Ilyŏng Kim, Ch'ŏl Kim and Yŏnghun Yi, 25–63. Seoul: Ch'aeksesang.

Yoon, Dae-Kyu. 2017. "The Constitution of North Korea: Its Changes and Implications". In *Public Law in East Asia*, 59–75. Routledge: London.

Yoon, Inshil Choe. 1996. "A Study and Translation of *T'aengniji*". PhD dissertation, University of Auckland.

Young, Benjamin. 2015. "Juche in the United States: The Black Panther Party's Relations with North Korea, 1969–1971". *Asia Pacific Journal (Japan Focus)* 13, no. 3. http://apjjf.org/2015/13/12/Benjamin-Young/4303.html.

Yu, Jong-ho. 1994. "The Mountain in Contemporary Fiction". *Koreana* 8, no. 4: 34–7.

Zajas, Krysztof. 2013. *Absent Culture: The Case of Polish Livonia*. Frankfurt and New York: Peter Lang.

# Index